one-dish
vegan

one-dish
vegan

More than 150 Soul-Satisfying Recipes
for Easy and Delicious One-Bowl and One-Plate Dinners

Robin Robertson

The Harvard Common Press
Boston, Massachusetts

To all those who work to make this a kinder, gentler world

The Harvard Common Press
www.harvardcommonpress.com

Copyright © 2013 by Robin Robertson

Printed in the United States of America
Printed on acid-free paper

Library of Congress Cataloging-in-Publication Data
Robertson, Robin (Robin G.)
    One-dish vegan : more than 150 soul-satisfying recipes for easy and delicious one-bowl and one-plate dinners / Robin Robertson.
        pages cm
    Includes index. 524467/2
    ISBN 978-1-55832-812-9 (alk. paper)
    1. Vegan cooking. 2. One-dish meals. I. Title.
    TX837.R62495 2013
    641.5'636--dc23

10/13

2013001297

Special bulk-order discounts are available on this and other Harvard Common Press books. Companies and organizations may purchase books for premiums or resale, or may arrange a custom edition, by contacting the Marketing Director at the address above.

Book design by Michelle Thompson | Fold & Gather Design
Front cover photograph by Danny Lerner; back cover photograph by Lori Maffei

Cover recipes, front: Brown Rice and White Beans with Shiitakes and Spinach (page 85); back: Risotto Primavera (page 66)

10 9 8 7 6 5 4 3 2

contents

acknowledgments

At the top of my list of people to thank are some of the best recipe testers a cookbook author could ever hope for. My gratitude goes to Barbara Bryan, Jonathan and Nancy Shanes, Lea Jacobson, Liz Wyman, Lori Maffei, Lyndsay Orwig, Melissa Chapman, Jessica Eiss, and Vegan Aide. Their dedication to testing every recipe and giving me helpful feedback along the way made my job a pleasure. I can't thank them enough.

Many thanks to the terrific team at The Harvard Common Press, especially Bruce Shaw, Dan Rosenberg, Adam Salomone, Virginia Downes, Pat Jalbert-Levine, Valerie Cimino, and Karen Wise, for their part in making this book a reality, as well as my longtime agent, Stacey Glick of Dystel & Goderich Literary Management.

I am also grateful, as always, to my husband, Jon, and our passel of cats, for their unconditional love and support, and for keeping me smiling.

introduction

We all know those certain special recipes that we return to again and again, particularly the satisfying one-dish family favorites that make us feel good all over. These are the recipes that are so flavorful that they taste like you've spent all day in the kitchen. That's what *One-Dish Vegan* is about—a comprehensive collection of vegan favorites filled with nourishing and delicious recipes for every season and every occasion.

One-dish meals are my favorite way to cook. Not only are they easy to make for weeknight dinners, but they're also ideal for serving company because they allow me to prepare meals in advance and then serve them from a clean kitchen. Another benefit that I especially appreciate on days when I'm too busy to cook is being able to prepare weeknight meals ahead to be reheated later.

One-Dish Vegan is an extensive revision of *One-Dish Vegetarian Meals*, which was a collection of favorite recipes drawn from some of my earlier books, namely *Rice & Spice, Pasta for All Seasons,* and *The Vegetarian Chili Cookbook,* along with many all-new recipes. While a number of the recipes in that previous book were already vegan, many included some dairy options. However, this new volume, *One-Dish Vegan,* now contains 100 percent vegan recipes. More than that, it is also "new and improved" in several other exciting ways, including:

- recipes that use less oil

- many recipes that are low in fat

- more recipes made with whole grains

- handy notations for gluten-free and soy-free dishes

- dozens of all-new recipes

Also included in this book is a clarification of the parameters of a "one-dish meal" as found in these recipes (see page 2). After *One-Dish Vegetarian Meals* was published, I discovered that people have varying interpretations of what constitutes a one-dish meal. I want to be clear that a one-dish meal doesn't necessarily mean one-pot preparation. Sometimes one-dish recipes require more than one pot or pan for advance prep, the components of which are then combined in a single pot, pan, or casserole in which the final dish is cooked and served.

One-Dish Vegan is filled with more than 150 great-tasting recipes that complement our busy lifestyles and our desire to eat healthful and great-tasting food without a lot of fuss. The dishes are economical, simple to prepare, and a pleasure to eat. They're also versatile and work equally well for simple weeknight dinners or for casual entertaining.

Many of the dishes can be made ahead and popped into the oven to heat just before mealtime, and they're great for feeding a crowd. They also lend themselves to easy transporting, making them ideal for potluck gatherings. These recipes for hearty comfort-food meals include satisfying soups, stews, and chili; lightning-quick stir-fries and sautés; comforting casseroles, lasagna, and baked stuffed vegetables; and pages of tempting pasta dishes and main-dish salads.

The globally inspired recipes in *One-Dish Vegan* offer tremendous variety and sophisticated flavors that will please vegans and omnivores alike, with choices such as Louisiana Red Beans and Rice, Three-Bean Quinoa Chili, Thai Peanut Bowl with Tofu and Asparagus, One-Pot Cheesy Mac, Frittata Puttanesca, Greek Gyro Salad, and many more.

Many of the recipes in this book have long been personal favorites of my family and friends. It is my hope that they will soon become your favorites as well.

in the kitchen

Before digging into the recipes, I'd like to share a few thoughts about the concept of this book and clarify what a one-dish meal means to me. I also want to offer some insights about the types of ingredients you'll be using to create these recipes and provide some professional cooking tips that will help you prepare delicious and satisfying meals with ease and confidence.

one-dish wonders

We all want to eat healthy, well-balanced meals, but we don't always have a lot of time to spend in the kitchen. That's why one-dish recipes can be especially appealing—the cooking methods are straightforward and simplified, and often the recipes can be assembled ahead of time, making for easy cleanup and less stress at mealtime.

I'd like to begin by answering this question: Does "one-dish" mean "one-pot"?

My answer to that is: oftentimes, yes it does, but not always. Let me explain. To me, a one-dish dinner is a meal that comes to the table in a single serving vessel. Sometimes that can mean it is prepared and served in the same pan or pot. Other times, two or more of the components of the meal are prepared separately and then combined before being served.

Here, then, are the guidelines I've used to distinguish the various types of one-dish-meal recipes that are contained in this book:

- Recipes in which all of the meal components—vegetables, grain, and protein—are cooked and served in one pot, skillet, or other vessel as a complete meal (such as hearty soups, stews, or stir-fries that contain a balance of vegetables, protein, and complex carbohydrates).

- Recipes in which the entire meal arrives at the table in a single pot, skillet, bowl, or dish, but which are not entirely prepared in that single vessel (such as cooking a separate sauce or sautéing a vegetable or other ingredient to add to the one-dish recipe). This category includes baked casseroles, where several components may be prepared separately and then combined into a single baking dish to bake and serve.

- Recipes that are generally best when rounded out by a simple accompaniment; most notably, those best served on a bed of either a cooked grain or pasta. This category also includes those recipes that I recommend serving with a salad. Obviously, such an accompaniment would require an additional vessel in which to prepare it.

By its very nature, this book is filled with main-dish recipes. You won't find any desserts, appetizers, or side dishes here. What you will find are loads of hearty and nutritious meals, including satisfying soups and stews, casseroles, and even main-dish salads. That said, when feeding a crowd, for example, you could certainly serve many of these recipes as part of a larger meal.

Even though many slow cooker recipes qualify as one-dish meals, there are no slow cooker recipes in this book simply because I've already written an entire book devoted to vegan slow cooker recipes. If you enjoy using a slow cooker, I invite you to explore *Fresh from the Vegan Slow Cooker* (The Harvard Common Press, 2012) .

a vegan kitchen

Because it is important to include a wide variety of beans, grains, vegetables, and other plant-based ingredients in a vegan diet, I have made a special effort to do so in these recipes—not just for their obvious nutritional value, but also to add interest and variety to your meals. Wherever possible, I've developed the recipes to include the three basic food groups most people like to find in their meals: vegetables, complex carbohydrates, and a good source of protein—aka "a green, a grain, and a bean." For any recipe that lacks one of those three elements, I suggest an easy accompaniment to serve with it.

about rice and other grains

Whole grains are an important part of any plant-based diet. An economical source of high-quality nutrition, grains are easy to digest, contain no cholesterol or saturated fat, and are rich in vitamins and minerals, making them a natural choice for healthy eating.

While rice is the most frequently featured grain in these recipes, several other wholesome grains are also used, including quinoa, barley, oats, and bulgur. Each type of grain has its own nutritional value, unique flavor, and cooking characteristics. When combined with beans, vegetables, and seasonings, grains provide great taste and texture, in addition to good nutrition. Once you begin cooking with a variety of grains, you'll significantly expand your recipe repertoire. For variety, try substituting a different grain for rice or pasta in a recipe. Grains can be used in soups, stuffings, pilafs, puddings, and desserts, as well as to make breads and pasta dishes.

Storing and Cooking Grains

Most whole raw grains can be stored unrefrigerated in tightly covered containers, as long as they are kept away from heat, light, and humidity. To prolong their shelf life, it's a good idea to store uncooked grains in the refrigerator or freezer.

Grains should be rinsed before using to remove loose hulls, dust, and other impurities. To intensify the flavor of a grain, you may toast it lightly in a dry skillet before cooking. For liquid amounts and cooking times for particular grains, see the chart that follows. If there is a grain not on that list that you would like to prepare, be aware that most grains can be cooked in a pot with about two times as much water as grain, or more, depending on the cooking time. Bring the water and grain to a boil, cover, reduce the heat to low, and simmer until tender, adding more water along the way if necessary. The water will be absorbed into the grain as it cooks. When the grain is tender, drain away any liquid left in the pot.

Since many grain varieties take 30 minutes or less to cook, a wholesome meal made with freshly cooked grains can be ready quickly. For grains that do require a longer cooking time or that you use frequently, I recommend cooking a large batch once a week and portioning it into meal-size containers that can be stored in the refrigerator or freezer. (If you own a pressure cooker, it is a great tool for preparing longer-cooking grains speedily.) Grains can be easily reheated without compromising taste or texture. Whether seasoned with toasted sesame oil, tamari, or grated ginger, or enlivened with lemon zest or fresh herbs, grains can easily adapt to most any ethnic flavor nuance that comes their way.

Grain Cooking Chart

The following chart shows stovetop cooking times and water amounts for the grains used in this book. To cook, combine the grain and water in a saucepan. Cover and bring to a boil. Reduce the heat to low, add salt to the water, and simmer, covered, until the water is absorbed. Soaking, altitude, and the age of the grain may all influence the outcome, so be sure to monitor and test for doneness. In each case, remove the pot from the heat at the end of the cooking time and allow the grain to rest, covered, for 5 minutes. Generally, 1 cup uncooked grain will yield 3 cups cooked.

GRAIN (1 CUP)	WATER	COOKING TIME
Barley	3 cups	1 hour
Buckwheat (kasha)	2½ cups	20 minutes
Bulgur	2 cups	15 minutes
Couscous	1½ cups	10 minutes
Millet	2 cups	30 minutes
Quinoa	2 cups	20 minutes
Rice:		
Basmati	2 cups	30–40 minutes
Jasmine	1¾ cups	15 minutes
Long-grain brown	2 cups	30–40 minutes
Short-grain brown	2½ cups	45–50 minutes
Sweet or sticky	1½ cups	15–20 minutes
Wild	2½ cups	45–50 minutes

about beans

Many of the recipes in this book call for beans of one kind or another. Many people prefer to cook with dried beans, while others enjoy the convenience of canned. For that reason, my recipes give you the option of using either cooked-from-scratch or canned beans. You can decide which works better for you. If you're using canned beans, seek out an organic variety, as they generally contain no additives. Be sure to rinse canned beans in cool water and then drain them before using. A drained 15.5-ounce can of beans yields approximately 1½ cups beans, so the amount of beans used in these recipes is often 1½ or 3 cups, to allow for canned beans to be used with ease.

Most dried beans need to be soaked in water prior to cooking. They can be quick-soaked in a pot of hot, boiled water for an hour, or they can be left covered in the refrigerator to soak overnight. I like to add a piece of kombu seaweed to the pot when cooking beans: While it won't affect the taste, kombu acts as a natural flavor enhancer and tenderizer, and it helps decrease the cooking time. It also adds important minerals and aids in digestion.

Bean Cooking Chart

Use this chart as a guideline for dried soaked beans cooked on the stovetop. Note that lentils and split peas do not require soaking prior to cooking. Cook beans with the lid on, stirring occasionally. Generally, 1 cup of dried beans will yield 2 to 2½ cups of cooked beans. Cooking times may vary depending on the type, quality, and age of the bean, the altitude, and even the water quality.

BEAN (1 CUP DRIED)	WATER	COOKING TIME
Adzuki beans	3 cups	50 minutes
Black beans	3½ cups	1½–2 hours
Black-eyed peas	3 cups	1 hour
Cannellini beans	3½ cups	1½–2 hours
Chickpeas	4 cups	3 hours
Great Northern beans	3½ cups	1½–2 hours
Kidney beans	3½ cups	2 hours
Lentils	3 cups	35–45 minutes
Navy beans	3½ cups	1½–2 hours
Pinto beans	3½ cups	2 hours
Split peas	3 cups	45 minutes

about tofu, tempeh, and seitan

In addition to beans, the other main plant-based protein sources are tofu, tempeh, and seitan. Here is some basic information about each.

TOFU: Tofu is a curd made from soybeans. Nutritionally, tofu is very high in protein, calcium, iron, and B-complex vitamins. Its inherent lack of flavor makes tofu a valuable ingredient for the imaginative cook because it readily absorbs other flavors and seasonings. It is available in different degrees of firmness, each of which is suitable for different types of dishes; for instance, I prefer extra-firm regular tofu for stir-fries, sautés, and similar recipes, while reserving silken tofu for recipes that call for pureeing. Before using any kind of tofu, drain it well, pressing out the excess water, and blot dry.

TEMPEH: Tempeh is made of fermented, compressed soybeans that are formed into firm cakes. Tempeh has a distinctive flavor and chewy texture and can be cubed, crumbled, or grated to resemble ground meat. It is high in protein and B vitamins, including vitamin B12. Tempeh can be found in the refrigerated section of natural foods stores and many supermarkets. For best results, I recommend that you steam tempeh before using it to mellow its flavor and also to make it more digestible. This simply means that you need to place it on a rack or in a steamer basket over boiling water for 15 minutes before using it as directed in the recipe.

SEITAN: Called "wheat meat" because it is made from wheat, seitan (pronounced "say-TAN") is a popular and versatile ingredient that can be ground, diced, cubed, or sliced. In addition to being a good source of protein, vitamin C, and iron, seitan is also low in fat and calories: One 4-ounce serving contains only 70 calories and 1 gram of fat. Made with vital wheat gluten and water (along with various seasonings), seitan is available ready-made in the refrigerated or freezer sections of most natural foods stores. However, because it can be expensive to buy and is easy to make at home, I recommend making your own seitan using the recipe that follows.

This is my go-to seitan recipe, which can be prepared in a variety of ways: on the stovetop, in a slow cooker, or in the oven. It's simple to make and much less expensive than commercially available seitan. Look for vital wheat gluten in natural foods stores or online.

1 ¾ cups vital wheat gluten

¼ cup white whole-wheat flour

½ cup nutritional yeast

1 teaspoon onion powder

½ teaspoon garlic powder

½ teaspoon salt

¼ teaspoon freshly ground black pepper

3 to 6 tablespoons wheat-free tamari

1 tablespoon olive oil

1 ¾ cups water

1. In a large bowl, combine the vital wheat gluten, flour, nutritional yeast, onion powder, garlic powder, salt, and pepper. Stir in 3 tablespoons of the tamari, the olive oil, and the water, and continue stirring until well mixed. Knead for 2 minutes to activate the gluten. Proceed with one of the following cooking methods:

   On the stovetop: Pour about 2 quarts water into a large pot. Divide the seitan dough into 4 pieces and add to the water along with the remaining 3 tablespoons tamari. Cover and bring to a simmer, but do not allow to boil. Uncover and simmer for 1 hour.

   In a slow cooker: Pour about 2 quarts water into a large slow cooker. Divide the seitan dough into 4 pieces and add to the water along with the remaining 3 tablespoons tamari. Cover and cook on LOW for 5 to 6 hours.

   In the oven: Preheat the oven to 350°F. Place the seitan dough on an oiled sheet of aluminum foil and enclose it in the foil. Place the wrapped seitan inside a large baking dish, seam side up. Add about an inch of water to the baking pan and cover the entire pan tightly with foil. Bake until firm, about 1 ¾ hours. (If using the oven method, you will not need the additional 3 tablespoons tamari.)

2. Transfer the cooked seitan to a baking sheet to cool. If you are not using the seitan right away, store, tightly wrapped, in the refrigerator for up to 5 days or in the freezer for several weeks. The cooking liquid may be reserved and used in sauces or frozen and used again the next time you make seitan.

MAKES ABOUT 1 ½ POUNDS

other plant-based proteins

Beyond beans, tofu, tempeh, and seitan are a number of commercially available products that have a "meaty" taste and texture. Usually a blend of soy and grains, along with flavorings, these products can be extremely helpful to the creative cook trying to please a diverse crowd. From prepared vegan sausage links to texturized vegetable protein (TVP), such ingredients are called for sparingly in this book, and generally there is an alternative listed for those who prefer not to use such products.

dairy-free foods

A wide variety of vegan milk and cheese products are available in supermarkets and natural foods stores. Popular nondairy milks are almond, soy, rice, and coconut milk. My personal preference for most recipes is plain unsweetened almond milk. Other convenient dairy-free products include vegan mayonnaise, sour cream, cream cheese, and yogurt. Vegan butter, including a soy-free version, can be found in well-stocked supermarkets.

A number of vegan cheeses are available as well, including vegan Parmesan, mozzarella, cheddar, and others that can be found shredded and in blocks. You will discover only sparse optional suggestions for using such products in this book. I prefer, instead, to use unprocessed ingredients. For example, ground nuts combined with a little salt makes for a flavorful Parmesan cheese alternative. Because of its salty, cheese-like flavor, I sometimes call for nutritional yeast in recipes that would benefit from its flavor.

You can also make easy homemade versions of some dairy products instead of buying them ready-made. There are recipes in this book for homemade vegan sour cream (page 101) and a cheddar-like cheese sauce (page 93).

vegetable broth

The use of vegetable broth to make soups and stews is a matter of personal taste. While it isn't always necessary to a recipe, it does add nutrients and an extra dimension of flavor. Making vegetable broth is not difficult, nor does it need to be time-consuming. It can be as easy as boiling water—all you have to do is add some vegetables to the water and walk away. After about an hour of simmering, you can strain out the vegetables, and the resulting liquid is your broth. Cook it longer, and the broth is richer.

An all-purpose vegetable broth made with little more than onions, carrots, celery, and water is a modest investment that will provide substantial dividends to your meals. When I make vegetable broth, I begin by sweating the vegetables in a little oil to deepen their flavors. I usually coarsely chop the vegetables, often keeping the skins, peels, stems, and leaves on for added flavor. Just be sure to wash all ingredients well before adding them to the pot.

Many of the soup and stew recipes in this book offer you a choice of using broth or water. In these cases, water will work just fine in the recipe, but using broth will result in a richer flavor; the choice is yours. An easy alternative to homemade broth that I use frequently is combining a good-quality vegetable soup base paste with water. There are also vegetable bouillon cubes and vegetable soup base powders that may be used in the same way. These products vary in flavor and saltiness, so be sure to taste them before using in a recipe so you know what to expect. You may need to experiment to find ones you like, and remember to adjust the seasonings in your recipes accordingly. Sometimes when I want to enrich the flavor of a particular dish, I add a splash of tamari or a little bit of dissolved miso paste.

The actual amount of salt you add to your homemade broth is up to you, but less is better than more. While salt does help bring out the flavor of the vegetables, adding too much salt will impair the flavor, especially if the broth is reduced further, which will intensify the saltiness. I usually begin by adding 1 teaspoon salt to my basic 6-cup broth recipe (page 10), then I adjust the seasoning toward the end of cooking, after the flavors have had a chance to develop.

BASIC VEGETABLE BROTH

Gluten-free | Soy-free option

Use this basic vegetable broth as a guideline. Feel free to add other vegetables or seasonings according to your personal preference, although it is best to omit boldly colored or strongly flavored vegetables that may be too pronounced.

2 teaspoons olive oil or ¼ cup water

1 large yellow onion, coarsely chopped

2 celery ribs, chopped

2 carrots, peeled and coarsely chopped

8 cups water

2 garlic cloves, crushed

½ cup coarsely chopped fresh Italian parsley

1 large bay leaf

½ teaspoon whole black peppercorns

1 tablespoon wheat-free tamari (optional)

Salt

1. Heat the oil or water in a large pot over medium heat. Add the onion, celery, and carrots, cover, and cook until slightly softened, about 5 minutes. Remove the lid and add the water, garlic, parsley, bay leaf, peppercorns, tamari (if using), and salt to taste. Bring to a boil, then reduce the heat to medium-low and simmer for 1 hour to reduce the liquid and bring out the flavors of the vegetables.

2. Strain the broth through a fine-mesh sieve into another pot, pressing the juices out of the vegetables with the back of a large spoon. The broth is now ready to use. For a more concentrated broth, return the broth to a boil, and reduce the volume by one-quarter. Stored tightly covered in the refrigerator, it will keep for up to 3 days. Alternatively, you may portion and freeze it for up to 4 months.

MAKES ABOUT 6 CUPS

about oils

I generally recommend keeping at least three varieties of oil on hand: extra-virgin olive oil for salads and most cooking, dark (toasted) sesame oil for adding flavor to certain Asian dishes, and a light-flavored neutral vegetable oil (I like grapeseed oil) for when you don't want the flavor of olive oil or sesame oil. High-quality, cold-pressed oils are always the best choice.

As I mentioned earlier, many of these recipes use very little oil or provide the option of using no added oil, if that is your preference. For stovetop cooking, try using a few tablespoons of water or vegetable broth instead of oil to keep ingredients from sticking to the pan. Another alternative is to use nonstick cookware. In the oven, nonstick bakeware or parchment paper can be used when roasting vegetables, or you might opt for using a small amount of nonstick cooking spray.

about chiles and chili powder

Since there is an entire chapter in this book devoted to chili recipes, a few words about chiles and chili powder seem in order. These days, many supermarkets carry a selection of both fresh and dried chile peppers, so experimenting can be fun. When handling chiles, it is best to wear rubber gloves, being careful not to touch your eyes, as the capsaicin oil will burn. Some of the hotter chiles even release fumes that are quite strong. Always wash your hands and gloves thoroughly in warm soapy water after handling chiles.

You can make your own chili powder blend using already ground dried chiles or dried whole chiles that you grind yourself; customize the blend by adding cumin and other seasonings such as oregano and paprika. Commercially available chili powders are generally a blend of ground chile peppers combined with cumin, oregano, garlic, and salt. These blends vary greatly in quality and flavor and can sometimes be stale or of inferior quality. In selecting a commercial powder blend, try to find one that consists only of ground chiles, oregano, and cumin. For the best flavor, try to steer clear of those containing garlic, salt, and other additives.

The following recipe is one of my favorite blends; you can use it whenever a recipe calls for chili powder, adjusting amounts as your preference for hot or mild dictates.

MEDIUM-HOT CHILI POWDER

Gluten-free | Soy-free

Use this as a guideline and experiment with different types and amounts of chiles to create your own signature blend. The other spice amounts may be adjusted as well.

2 dried cayenne chiles, stemmed and seeded

2 dried ancho chiles, stemmed and seeded

2 dried Anaheim chiles, stemmed and seeded

1 tablespoon whole cumin seeds

1 tablespoon paprika

1 teaspoon dried oregano

Cut the chiles into small pieces and place in a blender or spice mill. Add the cumin seeds, paprika, and oregano and grind into a fine powder. Store in an airtight container in a cool, dry place.

MAKES ABOUT 1½ CUPS

Note: If you prefer to begin with ground spices, here is a good ratio to start with, adjusting for hotter or milder to taste: Combine 1 cup mild ground dried chiles, ¼ cup hot ground dried chiles, 2 tablespoons ground cumin, and 2 tablespoons ground oregano.

other ingredients

Because the recipes in this book are inspired by numerous global cuisines, there may be some ingredients that you have never tried. Most of the ingredients used in these recipes can be found in any well-stocked supermarket. In the case of any unusual ingredient, I've done my best to list an alternative choice in case the first choice is unavailable in your location.

Like most health-conscious people, I believe that fresh, organic ingredients are best and that highly processed food is to be avoided. You will notice that my recipes call for tamari, a high-quality Japanese soy sauce, instead of regular soy sauce. This is because tamari does not contain the additives found in many brands of soy sauce. For the best quality, be sure to buy one that is labeled "wheat-free." For a soy-free alternative to tamari, try coconut aminos. I also recommend sea salt over regular table salt and favor natural sweeteners over white sugar.

Gluten-Free, Soy-Free, Low-Fat

With so many people looking for recipes that are gluten-free, soy-free, or low in fat, it's important to me that my recipes be accessible to as many people as possible, regardless of any dietary restrictions. For that reason, most of the recipes are naturally low in fat or sometimes even fat-free. For example, in many cases, a choice is given to sauté ingredients either in water or in a small amount of oil.

Many of the recipes are also gluten-free, soy-free, or both, and they are noted as such for quick reference. Wherever possible, easy substitutions are also noted to make a recipe either gluten-free or soy-free. For example, you may substitute gluten-free pasta for regular pasta or lima beans for edamame.

Recipes that are marked "gluten-free" do not contain common gluten ingredients such as seitan, wheat pasta, barley, or rye, and such recipes will call for gluten-free oats or wheat-free tamari. However, just as hidden animal ingredients can find their way into certain products, so too is the case with gluten and soy, so you need to maintain your own vigilance with regards to the particular products you buy.

Important: If you have a serious gluten sensitivity, read *all* labels carefully to be sure that the products you are buying are gluten-free. Certain commercially available products, such as hoisin sauce, vegetable broth, soup base paste, and bouillon cubes may contain gluten, although gluten-free versions are easily found in most markets. Because gluten-free versions of these products are so readily available, my recipes do not specifically call out such ingredients with regard to gluten content. If you are especially gluten-sensitive, be sure to double-check the ingredient labels of all products you use to be sure they contain no gluten. For information regarding gluten-free ingredients, visit www.celiac.com. Naturally, the same cautionary advice is also true for soy or other food allergies you may have.

Also, be aware that if I give a choice in the ingredient list (such as "nutritional yeast or white miso paste"), the gluten-free and soy-free recipe notations are based on use of the first ingredient option.

recipe yields and portion amounts

Deciding how many people a certain recipe will serve can be tricky. After all, we don't all eat the same amount at meals—some people have large appetites, while others prefer smaller portions. Factor in that the recipes may be served alone or with other dishes, and it is clear that the yield amount is meant to be a guideline and not a hard-and-fast rule.

Because this book is designed for "one-dish meals," the yield amounts lean to larger portions, the assumption being that the recipe in question is the complete meal itself or will be served with a minimal accompaniment such as salad or bread.

Most of the recipes in this book yield four servings. However, if you know that your family tends to eat smaller portions, or if you plan to serve a few other dishes or courses with a particular recipe, then you may be able to stretch six or more portions out of a recipe designed to feed four hearty appetites as a one-dish meal.

in the kitchen: a pantry postscript

If you enjoy the convenience and ease of preparing one-dish meals, then a well-stocked pantry can be a valuable asset. When your larder is full of the ingredients used in these recipes, you'll never again be stumped at dinnertime.

Include a range of dried or canned beans such as chickpeas, cannellini beans, lentils, kidney beans, and pintos. Stock your pantry with a variety of pasta, rice, and other grains, extra-virgin olive oil, and canned tomato products, including paste, puree, and diced and whole tomatoes. Keep on hand a supply of dried herbs, spices, sea salt, and other basic seasonings, as well as standard baking items such as flours, baking soda, baking powder, and extracts.

Line your shelves with olives, capers, sun-dried tomatoes, artichoke hearts, dried mushrooms, and roasted red peppers. For those times when you want to cook with an Asian flair, be sure to include tamari, toasted sesame oil, chili paste, sriracha sauce, fresh ginger, and other flavor enhancers.

A well-stocked kitchen should also include fresh staples such as onions, carrots, celery, lettuce and other salad ingredients, and a wide selection of vegetables and fruits, including fresh herbs whenever possible.

By keeping a variety of basic ingredients on hand, you'll always be ready to create nourishing and flavorful meals whenever you want them for yourself, your family, and your friends.

soups that make a meal

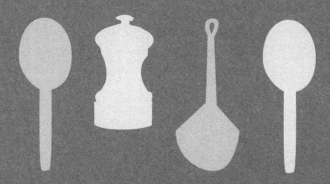

chickpea noodle soup

Gluten-free option | Soy-free

THIS COMFORTING, VERSATILE SOUP can be altered easily to suit your taste. For example, vary the vegetables according to personal preference, or substitute seitan, tempeh, or different beans for the chickpeas. As the noodles cook in the soup, they will absorb some of the broth, so you may want to add a little more broth before serving. Alternatively, if you have leftover cooked pasta from another meal, you can just add it when ready to serve instead of cooking the noodles right in the soup. To make this soup gluten-free, use gluten-free pasta and, of course, make sure that your vegetable broth is gluten-free.

2 teaspoons olive oil or ¼ cup water

1 medium-size yellow onion, chopped

2 carrots, peeled and thinly sliced

1 celery rib, thinly sliced

3 garlic cloves, minced

1 teaspoon dried basil

1 teaspoon dried thyme

7 cups vegetable broth, or more if needed

4 ounces green beans, trimmed and cut into 1-inch pieces

4 cups coarsely chopped stemmed kale or cabbage

3 cups cooked chickpeas or 2 (15.5-ounce) cans chickpeas, rinsed and drained

1 (14.5-ounce) can diced tomatoes, undrained

Salt and freshly ground black pepper

6 ounces uncooked linguine, broken into thirds

½ cup fresh or frozen peas

2 tablespoons minced fresh Italian parsley

1. Heat the oil or water in a large pot over medium heat. Add the onion, carrots, and celery, and cook for 5 minutes to soften. Stir in the garlic and cook for 1 minute longer, then add the basil, thyme, and broth and bring to a boil. Reduce the heat to a simmer and cook for 10 minutes.

2. Add the green beans, kale, chickpeas, and tomatoes with their juices. Season to taste with salt and pepper. Simmer until the vegetables are tender, about 20 minutes.

3. Stir in the pasta, peas, and parsley. Simmer until the pasta is tender, about 15 minutes longer. Taste and adjust the seasonings if needed. Serve hot.

SERVES 4

chunky vegetable soup

THIS IS ONE of those clean-out-your-refrigerator soups—you can include whatever fresh or frozen vegetables you happen to have on hand. If you have a small amount of leftover cooked rice or pasta in the fridge, divide it among your bowls and ladle the hot soup on top.

1 tablespoon olive oil or ¼ cup water

1 large yellow onion, diced

2 carrots, peeled and diced

1 rib celery, chopped

2 garlic cloves, minced

1 large Yukon gold potato, scrubbed or peeled, diced

1½ cups frozen lima beans

1 (14.5-ounce) can diced fire-roasted tomatoes, undrained

1½ cups cooked chickpeas or 1 (15.5-ounce) can chickpeas, rinsed and drained

2 tablespoons wheat-free tamari

1 teaspoon dried marjoram

1 teaspoon dried basil

¼ teaspoon red pepper flakes

6 cups vegetable broth

1 tablespoon minced fresh Italian parsley

Salt and freshly ground black pepper

1. Heat the oil or water in a large pot over medium heat. Add the onion, carrots, celery, and garlic, cover, and cook, stirring occasionally, until softened, about 5 minutes. Add the potato, limas, tomatoes with their juices, chickpeas, tamari, marjoram, basil, and red pepper flakes. Add the broth and bring to a boil, then reduce the heat to a simmer and cook until the vegetables are tender, about 30 minutes.

2. Stir in the parsley and season to taste with salt and pepper. Serve hot.

SERVES 4

my thai soup with asparagus

Gluten-free

DELICATE GRAINS OF JASMINE RICE absorb this flavorful broth, hot with chiles and tangy with lemongrass, ginger, and lime juice. If Thai basil is unavailable, substitute regular basil or cilantro.

6 cups water

1 teaspoon salt

2 inner stalks lemongrass, cut into
   1-inch lengths

2 serrano or other small hot chiles, seeded
   and thinly sliced

1 teaspoon grated fresh ginger

½ cup uncooked jasmine rice

8 ounces asparagus, trimmed and cut
   diagonally into 1-inch pieces

1 cup unsweetened coconut milk

1 tablespoon wheat-free tamari

12 to 14 ounces extra-firm tofu, well drained,
   blotted dry, and diced

3 scallions, minced

Juice of 1 lime

¼ cup coarsely chopped fresh Thai basil

1. In a large saucepan, combine the water, salt, lemongrass, chiles, and ginger. Bring to a boil, then reduce the heat and simmer for 20 minutes.

2. Strain the broth through a sieve, discard the aromatics, return the broth to the saucepan, and bring to a boil. Add the rice and cook for 15 minutes. Reduce the heat to low and add the asparagus, coconut milk, and tamari. Stir well and simmer until the rice and asparagus are tender, about 5 minutes. Stir in the tofu, scallions, and lime juice, then taste and adjust the seasonings if needed. Sprinkle with the basil and serve hot.

SERVES 4

black bean soup
with kale and sweet potatoes

CHOCK FULL OF COLORFUL VEGETABLES and hearty beans, this flavorful soup contains all the elements of a satisfying and delicious meal.

1 tablespoon olive oil or ¼ cup water

1 medium-size yellow onion, finely chopped

3 garlic cloves, minced

1 large sweet potato, peeled and cut into
½-inch dice

3 cups cooked black beans or 2 (15.5-ounce)
cans black beans, rinsed and drained

1 (14.5-ounce) can diced tomatoes with chiles,
undrained

1 teaspoon ground cumin

½ teaspoon ground coriander

½ teaspoon smoked paprika

4 cups vegetable broth

Salt and freshly ground black pepper

6 cups chopped stemmed kale

3 tablespoons minced fresh cilantro
(optional)

1. Heat the oil or water in a large pot over medium heat. Add the onion and cook until softened, about 5 minutes. Add the garlic and cook for 1 minute longer. Stir in the sweet potato, beans, tomatoes with their juices, cumin, coriander, paprika, vegetable broth, and salt and pepper to taste. Bring to a boil, then reduce the heat to medium and simmer until the vegetables are almost tender, about 20 minutes.

2. Stir in the kale and cilantro, if using. Taste and adjust the seasonings if needed. Cook for another 10 minutes or until the vegetables are tender. Serve hot.

SERVES 4

pesto-enhanced vegetable soup

THE RICH VEGETABLE SOUP known as minestrone is popular throughout Italy. In both Milan and Genoa, a swirl of pesto is added near the end of cooking time to enrich the soup, but the addition of yellow bell pepper is strictly Calabrese. To make this soup gluten-free, use gluten-free pasta.

1 tablespoon olive oil or ¼ cup water

1 large onion, minced

1 or 2 carrots, peeled and cut into ¼-inch slices

3 garlic cloves, minced

1 yellow bell pepper, seeded and chopped

1 (14.5-ounce) can diced fire-roasted tomatoes, undrained

2 tablespoons tomato paste

4 cups chopped escarole, stemmed kale, or cabbage

1 teaspoon dried basil

½ teaspoon dried oregano

7 cups vegetable broth

Salt and freshly ground black pepper

1 medium-size zucchini, cut into ¼-inch dice

1½ cups cooked chickpeas or 1 (15.5-ounce) can chickpeas, rinsed and drained

⅓ cup uncooked ditalini or other small soup pasta

¼ cup Basil Pesto (recipe follows)

1. Heat the oil or water in a large pot over medium heat, and add the onion, carrots, and garlic. Cook for 5 minutes to soften. Add the bell pepper, tomatoes with their juices, tomato paste, escarole, basil, oregano, and broth. Bring to a boil, then reduce the heat to a simmer and cook for 20 minutes.

2. Season to taste with salt and pepper. Stir in the zucchini and chickpeas and cook for 10 minutes. Add the ditalini and cook until the pasta and vegetables are tender, about 8 minutes longer.

3. Swirl the pesto into the pot of soup, or ladle the soup into bowls and top each serving with a small spoonful of the pesto. Serve hot.

SERVES 4

BASIL PESTO

3 garlic cloves, crushed

½ teaspoon salt

⅓ cup lightly toasted pine nuts, walnuts,
   or almonds

2 cups fresh basil leaves

¼ cup olive oil

Combine the garlic and salt in a food processor and process to a paste. Add the pine nuts, basil, and oil and process until smooth and combined. For a thinner pesto, add more oil or a small amount of water or vegetable broth.

MAKES ABOUT 1 ½ CUPS

wild watercress soup
with slivers of seitan

WILD RICE AND WOODSY MUSHROOMS are a natural combination, and the touch of thyme enhances the rich flavors in this simple but elegant soup. The watercress is added near the end of the cooking time so it retains its fresh taste and vivid color, while the addition of hearty seitan makes this soup meal-worthy. To make this gluten-free, omit the seitan and add diced tofu or cooked white beans instead.

1 tablespoon olive oil or ¼ cup water

1 medium-size onion, minced

2 celery ribs, minced

⅓ cup uncooked wild rice

7 cups vegetable broth

½ teaspoon salt

⅛ teaspoon cayenne pepper

1 tablespoon chopped fresh thyme or 1 teaspoon dried thyme

1 bay leaf

⅓ cup uncooked basmati rice

8 ounces mushrooms, preferably shiitake (stemmed) or cremini, sliced

8 ounces watercress, thick stems removed, chopped

6 ounces seitan, cut into thin slivers

1. Heat the oil or water in a large saucepan over medium heat. Add the onion and celery and cook until softened, about 5 minutes. Stir in the wild rice, then add the broth, salt, and cayenne and bring to a boil. Reduce the heat to low, add the dried thyme (if using) and the bay leaf, cover, and simmer for 35 minutes.

2. Add the basmati rice and mushrooms and simmer for 30 minutes longer.

3. Stir in the watercress, seitan, and fresh thyme (if using) and cook until the rice is tender, about 10 minutes. Taste and adjust the seasonings if needed, discard the bay leaf, and serve hot.

SERVES 4

caribbean greens and beans soup

Gluten-free | Soy-free

THIS SOUP IS INSPIRED BY a delicious Jamaican soup made with callaloo (taro) leaves in a light coconut broth. My version calls for the more readily available spinach, although cabbage, kale, or chard may be used instead. The soup has a nice heat from the jalapeños, but you can omit them for a milder flavor or increase them if you want more heat.

1 tablespoon olive oil or ¼ cup water

1 medium-size red onion, chopped

3 garlic cloves, chopped

2 medium-size sweet potatoes, peeled and diced

1 medium-size red bell pepper, seeded and chopped

1 or 2 jalapeños or other hot chiles, seeded and minced

1 (14.5-ounce) can diced tomatoes, drained

1½ cups cooked dark red kidney beans or 1 (15.5-ounce) can dark red kidney beans, rinsed and drained

4 cups vegetable broth

2 teaspoons fresh thyme or 1 teaspoon dried thyme

¼ teaspoon ground allspice

Salt and freshly ground black pepper

9 ounces baby spinach

1 (13.5-ounce) can unsweetened coconut milk

1. Heat the oil or water in a pot over medium-high heat. Add the onion and sauté for 5 minutes. Add the garlic and cook for 1 minute longer. Add the sweet potatoes, bell pepper, jalapeño, tomatoes, and beans. Stir in the broth, thyme, and allspice, and season to taste with salt and pepper. Bring to a boil, then reduce the heat to a simmer and cook until the vegetables are tender, about 30 minutes.

2. Stir in the spinach and coconut milk, stirring to wilt the spinach. Taste and adjust the seasonings. Cook for 5 to 10 minutes longer to wilt the spinach and blend the flavors. Taste and adjust the seasonings if needed. Serve hot.

SERVES 4

mushroom and quinoa soup

CREAMY WHITE BEANS AND QUINOA combine with juicy mushroom slices for a luscious, protein-rich soup that makes a satisfying lunch or light supper.

1 tablespoon olive oil or ¼ cup water

1 large yellow onion, chopped

2 carrots, peeled and chopped

3 cups finely shredded napa cabbage

1 cup uncooked quinoa, rinsed and drained

5 cups mushroom or vegetable broth

3 tablespoons dry white wine, sherry, or mirin

1 tablespoon minced fresh thyme or 1 teaspoon dried thyme

½ teaspoon porcini powder (optional)

12 ounces white mushrooms, thinly sliced (about 3 cups)

1½ cups cooked white beans or 1 (15.5-ounce) can white beans, rinsed and drained

2 tablespoons minced fresh Italian parsley

Salt and freshly ground black pepper

1. Heat the oil or water in a large pot over medium heat. Add the onion, carrots, and cabbage and cook, stirring occasionally, until softened, about 5 minutes. Add the quinoa, broth, wine, and dried thyme (if using). Bring to a boil, then reduce the heat to a simmer and cook, covered, for 20 minutes.

2. Stir in the porcini powder (if using), mushrooms, beans, fresh thyme (if using), and parsley. Season to taste with salt and pepper and cook until the mushrooms are tender, about 10 minutes. Serve hot.

SERVES 4

senegalese-inspired
red lentil soup

REMINISCENT OF THE CURRIED SOUPS of Senegal, this tasty potage combines lentils and sweet potatoes with cabbage and tomatoes for a delicious mingling of flavors and textures.

1 tablespoon vegetable oil or ¼ cup water	¼ teaspoon cayenne pepper
1 large yellow onion, chopped	1 large sweet potato, peeled and diced
1 carrot, peeled and chopped	2 cups shredded or chopped cabbage
2 garlic cloves, minced	1 (14.5-ounce) can diced tomatoes, undrained
1 cup dried red lentils	5 cups vegetable broth
2 tablespoons curry powder	Salt
½ teaspoon ground coriander	Chopped unsalted roasted peanuts or cashews, for garnish

1. Heat the oil or water in a large pot over medium heat. Add the onion and carrot and cook for 5 minutes. Stir in the garlic, lentils, curry powder, coriander, cayenne, sweet potato, cabbage, and tomatoes with their juices. Add the broth and bring to a boil. Reduce the heat to a simmer, add salt to taste, and cook, stirring occasionally, until the lentils and vegetables are soft, about 30 minutes. If the soup becomes too thick, stir in additional broth.

2. Serve hot, garnished with peanuts.

SERVES 4

minestrone with
cannellini beans and rice

THIS RECIPE UNITES BROWN RICE and cannellini beans in an herbaceous vegetable soup that is especially good served with warm garlic bread.

1 tablespoon olive oil or ¼ cup water

1 medium-size onion, minced

2 carrots, peeled and diced

3 garlic cloves, minced

½ cup uncooked long-grain brown rice

1 (14.5-ounce) can diced tomatoes, drained

7 cups vegetable broth

1 bay leaf

1 tablespoon minced fresh basil or 1 teaspoon dried basil

1 teaspoon minced fresh oregano or ½ teaspoon dried oregano

½ teaspoon minced fresh thyme or ¼ teaspoon dried thyme

8 ounces green beans, trimmed and cut into 2-inch pieces

2 medium-size zucchini, diced

1½ cups cooked cannellini beans or 1 (15.5-ounce) can cannellini beans, rinsed and drained

1 teaspoon salt

⅛ teaspoon freshly ground black pepper

¼ cup minced fresh Italian parsley

1. Heat the oil or water in a large pot over medium heat. Add the onion, carrots, and garlic and cook, stirring frequently, until the vegetables begin to soften, about 5 minutes. Add the rice, tomatoes, broth, bay leaf, and the dried basil, oregano, and thyme (if using), and bring to a boil. Reduce the heat to a simmer, cover, and cook for 15 minutes.

2. Stir in the green beans and cook until the rice is just tender, about 20 minutes longer.

3. Stir in the zucchini and cannellini beans, salt, and pepper and simmer for 10 minutes. Taste and adjust the seasonings if needed. Remove the bay leaf, then stir in the parsley, and the fresh basil, oregano, and thyme (if using). Serve hot.

SERVES 4 TO 6

red bean gumbo

Gluten-free | Soy-free

THE WORD *GUMBO* is an African word for okra, a traditional ingredient in this hearty vegetable soup. Although some versions of gumbo are made with just a small amount of rice, I prefer it thick with rice and served as a more substantial stew-like dish. The filé powder, made from ground sassafras leaves, helps to thicken this. Be sure to place a bottle of Tabasco sauce on the table so your guests can spice up the gumbo to their liking.

1 tablespoon olive oil or ¼ cup water

1 medium-size onion, diced

1 green bell pepper, seeded and diced

½ cup chopped celery

3 garlic cloves, minced

½ cup uncooked long-grain brown rice

6 cups vegetable broth or water

1 (14.5-ounce) can diced fire-roasted tomatoes, undrained

1½ cups cooked dark red kidney beans or 1 (15.5-ounce) can dark red kidney beans, rinsed and drained

1½ cups sliced fresh or frozen okra

½ teaspoon filé powder

1 teaspoon dried thyme

1 teaspoon salt

¼ teaspoon freshly ground black pepper

⅛ teaspoon cayenne pepper

Tabasco or other hot sauce, for serving

1. Heat the oil or water in a large saucepan over medium heat. Add the onion, bell pepper, celery, and garlic, and cook, stirring occasionally, until softened, about 5 minutes. Stir in the rice, broth, tomatoes with their juices, beans, okra, filé powder, thyme, salt, black pepper, and cayenne and bring to a boil. Reduce the heat to a simmer and cook, stirring occasionally, until the rice and vegetables are tender, about 35 minutes.

2. Taste and adjust the seasonings if needed. Serve hot, with hot sauce on the side.

SERVES 4

korean hot pot

PREVALENT THROUGHOUT ASIA, a hot pot is a one-pot meal in which the ingredients are simmered together in a broth. This particular version features a Korean flavor punctuated by the spicy chili paste known as *gochujang*. If you are gluten-sensitive, be sure to read the labels to find a gluten-free brand. After cooking, the pot is brought to the table for everyone to gather around and serve themselves, usually with cooked rice and condiments such as tamari and toasted sesame seeds to add at the table.

1 pound napa cabbage or bok choy, thinly sliced

1 carrot, peeled and cut into 2-inch pieces, then cut lengthwise into thin strips

4 ounces shiitake mushrooms, stemmed and thinly sliced

8 ounces extra-firm tofu, well drained, blotted dry, and cut into ½-inch dice

5 or 6 scallions, cut diagonally into 1-inch pieces

1 ounce enoki mushrooms, trimmed

2 cups fresh bean sprouts

1 (1-inch) piece peeled fresh ginger, thinly sliced

3 tablespoons wheat-free tamari

2 tablespoons *gochujang* or other Asian chili paste

1 tablespoon dark sesame oil

6 cups vegetable broth

Salt

Hot cooked rice, for serving

Wheat-free tamari, toasted sesame seeds, *gochujang*, and/or dark sesame oil, for serving

1. In a large pot, arrange the cabbage, carrot, shiitake mushrooms, tofu, scallions, enoki mushrooms, and bean sprouts in separate groups. Distribute the ginger slices among the other ingredients in the pot.

2. In a small bowl, combine the tamari, *gochujang*, and sesame oil. Mix well, then pour over the vegetables. Slowly add the broth. Cover and cook over medium heat until the ingredients are cooked, about 20 minutes. Taste the broth and add salt, if needed.

3. To serve, bring the pot to the dining table immediately. Place some hot cooked rice in the bottom of four soup bowls. Allow diners to serve themselves from the hot pot, transferring some of the various ingredients into their own bowls and garnishing as desired with their choice of tamari, sesame seeds, *gochujang*, and sesame oil. The remaining broth may be ladled into small cups or bowls to serve with the meal, if desired.

SERVES 4

creamy bean and winter vegetable soup

THIS SMOOTH, CREAMY SOUP provides an elegant change from the more rustic chunky vegetable and bean soups. If you prefer a chunky version, however, you can skip the pureeing step and serve the soup as is.

1 tablespoon olive oil or ¼ cup water

1 large yellow onion, diced

1 carrot, peeled and chopped

1 small rib celery, minced

2 garlic cloves, chopped

1 Yukon Gold or other potato, peeled and diced

½ butternut squash, peeled, seeded, and diced (about 2 cups)

1 (14.5-ounce) can fire-roasted diced tomatoes, undrained

½ teaspoon dried marjoram

½ teaspoon dried thyme

1½ cups cooked white beans or 1 (15.5-ounce) can white beans, rinsed and drained

5 cups vegetable broth

Salt and freshly ground black pepper

1 cup plain unsweetened nondairy milk (optional)

Minced fresh Italian parsley or chives, for garnish

1. Heat the oil or water in a large saucepan over medium heat. Add the onion, carrot, and celery and cook, covered, until softened, about 5 minutes. Add the garlic, potato, squash, tomatoes with their juices, marjoram, and thyme. Stir in the beans and broth and bring to a boil. Reduce the heat to a simmer and cook until the vegetables are tender, about 20 minutes. Remove from the heat and season to taste with salt and pepper.

2. Puree the soup mixture, in batches, in a food processor or high-speed blender until smooth, and return to the saucepan. Reheat slowly over low heat, stirring occasionally. Taste and adjust the seasonings if needed. Stir in the nondairy milk, if using, for added creaminess. Sprinkle with the parsley and serve hot.

SERVES 4

shiitake miso soup

MISO IS A RICH JAPANESE SOYBEAN PASTE that is said to have many healing properties. Be sure not to boil the soup once the miso paste has been added, since boiling destroys valuable enzymes. The addition of cooked brown rice and tofu just before serving makes this delicate soup substantial enough for a meal.

6 cups water

8 ounces shiitake mushrooms, stemmed and sliced

4 cups chopped napa cabbage

1 teaspoon grated fresh ginger

1 tablespoon wheat-free tamari

6 scallions, chopped

1 small carrot, peeled and finely shredded

3 tablespoons mellow white miso paste

12 ounces firm silken tofu, well drained, blotted dry, and diced

2 cups cooked brown rice

1. Bring the water to a boil in a medium-size saucepan over high heat. Add the mushrooms, cabbage, ginger, and tamari, reduce the heat to medium, and simmer for 10 minutes. Stir in the scallions and carrot and cook for 5 minutes longer.

2. Reduce the heat to low. Transfer about ¼ cup of the hot soup to a small bowl and add the miso paste, blending well. Stir the blended miso back into the soup and simmer for 2 minutes, being careful not to boil. Stir in the tofu and the cooked rice. Serve hot.

SERVES 4

lentil and butternut soup

NUTRIENT-RICH DARK GREENS, butternut squash, and lentils combine for a colorful wintertime soup with a rich, complex flavor.

1 tablespoon olive oil or ¼ cup water

1 medium-size onion, minced

1 celery rib, minced

3 garlic cloves, minced

2 tablespoons tomato paste

1 cup dried brown lentils, rinsed and picked over

1 (14.5-ounce) can fire-roasted diced tomatoes, undrained

½ teaspoon dried marjoram

7 cups vegetable broth

Salt and freshly ground black pepper

1 small butternut squash, peeled, seeded, and diced (about 3 cups)

4 cups coarsely chopped stemmed chard, kale, or other leafy greens

1 teaspoon minced fresh thyme or ½ teaspoon dried thyme

1. Heat the oil or water in a pot over medium heat. Add the onion, celery, and garlic. Cook for 5 minutes to soften. Stir in the tomato paste, then add the lentils, tomatoes with their juices, marjoram, and broth, and season to taste with salt and pepper. Bring to a boil, then reduce the heat and simmer for 20 minutes.

2. Add the squash and cook for 15 minutes longer. Stir in the greens and thyme, and simmer until the lentils and vegetables are tender, about 10 more minutes. Taste and adjust the seasonings if needed. Serve hot.

SERVES 4 TO 6

tuscan pasta and bean soup

THE PEOPLE OF TUSCANY are known as "bean eaters" because beans are an important component of their cooking. In addition to the creamy cannellini bean, Tuscans favor chickpeas, favas, and borlotti beans, which are also known as cranberry or Roman beans. The addition of zucchini makes this a one-dish meal, although a crisp green salad would be a terrific accompaniment, as would some warm garlic bread. For gluten-free, use gluten-free pasta and, of course, be sure to check that your vegetable broth is gluten-free.

1 tablespoon olive oil or ¼ cup water

1 medium-size yellow onion, minced

3 garlic cloves, minced

1 (6-ounce) can tomato paste

½ teaspoon dried oregano

½ teaspoon dried basil

½ teaspoon red pepper flakes (optional)

6 cups vegetable broth, or more if needed

1 bay leaf

Salt and freshly ground black pepper

1½ cups uncooked elbow macaroni or other small pasta such as ditalini

2 medium-size zucchini, cut into ¼-inch dice

3 cups cooked borlotti or cannellini beans or 2 (15.5-ounce) cans borlotti or cannellini beans, rinsed and drained

2 tablespoons minced fresh Italian parsley

1. Heat the oil or water in a large pot over medium heat. Add the onion and cook for 5 minutes to soften. Add the garlic and cook, stirring, for 1 minute. Blend in the tomato paste, oregano, basil, and red pepper flakes (if using). Stir in the broth. Add the bay leaf and salt and pepper to taste and bring to a boil. Reduce the heat to medium and simmer for about 20 minutes.

2. Return to a boil and stir in the macaroni, zucchini, and beans. Reduce the heat to a simmer and cook until the macaroni and zucchini are just tender, about 10 minutes. Add a little more broth, if needed. Remove the bay leaf, then taste and adjust the seasonings if needed. Stir in the parsley and serve hot.

SERVES 4 TO 6

spicy peanut soup

PEANUT BUTTER AND COCONUT MILK blend harmoniously with ginger, lime juice, and chiles in a sublime soup made substantial with tofu and rice. A fragrant jasmine or basmati would complement the delightful flavor and aroma of this soup. *Kecap manis*, a sweet, thick soy sauce, is available at Asian markets. (If you're gluten-sensitive, check the label to be sure it's gluten-free.) For a mild soup, omit the chiles. For a spicier soup, add some sriracha sauce when ready to serve.

1 tablespoon vegetable oil or ¼ cup water

1 medium-size onion, chopped

1 red bell pepper, seeded and chopped

2 garlic cloves, minced

1 or 2 small hot chiles, seeded and minced

2 teaspoons grated fresh ginger

⅓ cup peanut butter

2 tablespoons *kecap manis*, or 1½ tablespoons wheat-free tamari plus 1½ teaspoons molasses or natural sugar

1 (14.5-ounce) can diced tomatoes, undrained

½ cup uncooked jasmine rice

1 small head bok choy, thinly sliced (about 3 cups)

4 cups vegetable broth

8 ounces extra-firm tofu, well drained, blotted dry, and cut into ½-inch dice

1 cup unsweetened coconut milk

1 tablespoon freshly squeezed lime juice

Salt and freshly ground black pepper

¼ cup chopped unsalted roasted peanuts

1. Heat the oil or water in a large saucepan over medium heat. Add the onion, bell pepper, garlic, chile, and ginger and cook, stirring occasionally, until soft, about 5 minutes. Stir in the peanut butter, *kecap manis*, and tomatoes with their juices. Stir in the rice and bok choy, then add the broth. Bring to a boil, then reduce the heat to a simmer and cook until the vegetables and rice are tender and the flavors are well blended, about 20 minutes.

2. Stir in the tofu, coconut milk, and lime juice, and season to taste with salt and pepper. Simmer until heated through, about 5 minutes. Taste and adjust the seasonings if needed. Serve hot, sprinkled with the chopped peanuts.

SERVES 4

indonesian noodle soup with tofu

INSPIRED BY A HEADY INDONESIAN SOUP known as *laksa*, this luscious noodle soup is generally quite spicy, but you can tone it down by using less chili paste—or make it hotter by adding a bit more.

1 small yellow onion, diced

1 tablespoon Asian chili paste (or to taste)

1 tablespoon curry powder

2 teaspoons grated fresh ginger

1 teaspoon ground coriander

4½ cups vegetable broth

1 tablespoon vegetable oil or ¼ cup water

1 small head bok choy, chopped (about 3 cups)

4 scallions, minced

½ cup fresh or frozen peas

8 ounces extra-firm tofu, well drained, blotted dry, and cut into ½-inch dice

1 teaspoon wheat-free tamari

1½ teaspoons natural sugar

1 teaspoon salt

¼ teaspoon freshly ground black pepper

1 (13.5-ounce) can unsweetened coconut milk

6 ounces rice noodles, soaked and drained

2 tablespoons freshly squeezed lime juice

1 cup fresh bean sprouts

¼ cup coarsely chopped fresh cilantro

1. Combine the onion, chili paste, curry powder, ginger, coriander, and ½ cup of the broth in a food processor, and process until smooth.

2. Heat the oil or water in a large pot over medium heat. Add the onion mixture and cook, stirring, for 1 to 2 minutes. Watch carefully so it does not burn. Stir in the remaining 4 cups broth and bring to a boil. Reduce the heat to medium, add the bok choy, scallions, peas, tofu, tamari, sugar, salt, and pepper, and simmer for 5 minutes. Add the coconut milk and noodles, and simmer for 10 minutes longer.

3. Stir in the lime juice, then taste and adjust the seasonings if needed. Serve hot, topping each bowl with some of the bean sprouts and cilantro.

SERVES 4

main-dish salads

greek gyro salad

ALL THE FLAVORS OF A GYRO sandwich in a refreshing salad! Serve with warm pita bread for a satisfying meal. To make this soy-free, use a soy-free vegan yogurt.

2 garlic cloves, chopped

½ small cucumber, peeled, seeded, and quartered

Salt

½ cup plain vegan yogurt

3 tablespoons freshly squeezed lemon juice

2 tablespoons chopped fresh dill, mint, or Italian parsley

Freshly ground black pepper

1 tablespoon olive oil

8 ounces seitan, thinly sliced

1 teaspoon dried oregano

1 teaspoon dried rosemary

2 tablespoons red wine vinegar

½ teaspoon natural sugar

1 medium-size head romaine lettuce, finely chopped (about 6 cups)

½ small red onion, minced

1 rib celery, sliced

1 large tomato, chopped

1. In a food processor, combine the garlic, cucumber, and ½ teaspoon salt. Process to a paste. Add the yogurt, 1 tablespoon of the lemon juice, the dill, and salt and pepper to taste. Process until well blended, then taste and adjust the seasonings if needed, and set aside.

2. Heat the oil in a skillet over medium heat. Add the seitan and cook until browned, about 5 minutes. Add the oregano and rosemary, and season to taste with salt and pepper. Add the vinegar, sugar, and remaining 2 tablespoons lemon juice, tossing to coat.

3. To assemble, arrange the lettuce in the bottom of a large serving bowl. Add the seitan mixture, onion, celery, and tomato. Drizzle on as much of the dressing as you want and toss to coat. Serve immediately.

SERVES 4

antipasto potato salad

POTATO SALAD, ITALIAN-STYLE: That's what you get when you combine chunks of cooked potatoes with marinated artichoke hearts, roasted red bell peppers, capers, olives, and fresh and sun-dried tomatoes. There are chickpeas for protein, so you can spoon it over lettuce and dinner is served.

1 ½ pounds Yukon gold or new potatoes, peeled or scrubbed, cut into 1-inch chunks

1 (8-ounce) jar marinated artichoke hearts, drained and quartered

½ cup kalamata olives, pitted and halved

⅓ cup reconstituted or oil-packed sun-dried tomatoes, cut into thin strips

1 celery rib, minced

2 scallions, minced

½ roasted red bell pepper, chopped

1 ½ cups cooked chickpeas or 1 (15.5-ounce) can chickpeas, rinsed and drained

Salt and freshly ground black pepper

8 cherry or grape tomatoes, halved lengthwise

¼ cup minced fresh Italian parsley or basil

1 to 2 teaspoons capers (chopped if large)

2 tablespoons chopped fresh basil

2 garlic cloves, minced

2 tablespoons white wine vinegar

3 tablespoons olive oil

Torn salad greens, for serving

1. Cook the potatoes in a large pot of salted boiling water until just tender, about 15 minutes. Drain well and transfer to a large serving bowl.

2. Add the artichokes, olives, sun-dried tomatoes, celery, scallions, bell pepper, chickpeas, and salt and pepper to taste to the bowl with the potatoes. Add the cherry tomatoes, parsley, capers, and basil.

3. In a small bowl, combine the garlic, vinegar, oil, and salt and pepper to taste. Stir well to blend, then pour the dressing over the vegetables and toss gently to combine. Taste and adjust the seasonings if needed.

4. Arrange the salad greens on plates, top with the potato mixture, and serve.

SERVES 4

smoky chickpea salad with mango and avocado

Gluten-free

ROASTED CHICKPEAS WERE A FAVORITE SNACK of my Italian grandmother, who first introduced me to the savory, protein-rich treat many years ago. These days you can find numerous spin-offs of classic roasted chickpeas that cloak the chickpeas with various spice blends and sauces from curry to tamari. This one takes a smoky route. Once roasted, the chickpeas take on a lovely mahogany color and a deep smoky flavor that complements the other salad components. The luscious mango dressing can be made with your choice of Dijon mustard or sriracha sauce, either of which brings its own unique flavor note to the salad.

SMOKY CHICKPEAS:

1 tablespoon pure maple syrup

1 tablespoon wheat-free tamari

2 teaspoons liquid smoke

2 teaspoons olive oil

1 teaspoon nutritional yeast

1 teaspoon smoked paprika

½ teaspoon onion powder

¼ teaspoon freshly ground black pepper

¼ teaspoon salt

1½ cups cooked chickpeas or 1 (15.5-ounce) can chickpeas, rinsed and drained

DRESSING:

1 small mango, pitted, peeled, and chopped

3 tablespoons freshly squeezed lime juice

1 to 2 tablespoons agave nectar or pure maple syrup

2 teaspoons Dijon mustard or ½ teaspoon sriracha sauce

½ teaspoon liquid smoke

Salt and freshly ground black pepper

SALAD:

8 ounces spinach or watercress (or a combination), thick stems removed

1 mango

1 ripe Hass avocado

1. *For the smoky chickpeas:* Preheat the oven to 375°F. Line a shallow baking dish with parchment paper or spray it with nonstick cooking spray.

2. Place all of the chickpea ingredients in a bowl and toss to combine and coat the chickpeas. Transfer the chickpeas to the prepared baking dish and spread them out in a single layer. Bake for 30 minutes, stirring once about halfway through. The chickpeas should be lightly browned and nicely glazed. The chickpeas can be made in advance of the salad, if desired. Store in a tightly sealed container in the refrigerator for up to 3 days.

3. *For the dressing:* Combine the chopped mango, lime juice, agave, mustard, and liquid smoke in a high-speed blender or food processor. Blend until smooth, adding 1 to 3 tablespoons of water as needed to achieve the desired consistency. Season lightly with salt and pepper and blend again, then taste and adjust the seasonings if needed.

4. *For the salad:* Place the greens in a large salad bowl or mound onto individual plates. Top with the chickpeas. Pit, peel, and dice the mango and avocado, or use a small melon baller to scoop them into balls, then add them to the watercress and chickpeas. Drizzle the dressing onto the salad or serve the dressing on the side.

SERVES 4

pasta niçoise salad

NIÇOISE SALAD TAKES A TASTY TWIST when pasta is subbed in for potatoes. This great-tasting Mediterranean salad is an ideal one-dish meal for warm-weather al fresco dining. The salad is best made with thin young green beans, and cannellini beans stand in for the traditional tuna. To make this gluten-free, use gluten-free pasta.

12 ounces uncooked penne or other bite-size pasta

8 ounces green beans, trimmed

1½ tablespoons white wine vinegar

1½ tablespoons freshly squeezed lemon juice

1 tablespoon minced shallot

1 teaspoon Dijon mustard

½ teaspoon salt

¼ teaspoon natural sugar

Freshly ground black pepper

¼ cup olive oil

1½ cups cooked cannellini beans or 1 (15.5-ounce) can cannellini beans, rinsed and drained

¼ cup minced fresh Italian parsley

2 scallions, minced

Torn mixed salad greens, for serving

1½ cups cherry tomatoes, halved lengthwise

½ cup niçoise or kalamata olives, pitted

1 (6-ounce) jar marinated artichoke hearts, drained

1. Cook the penne in a large pot of boiling salted water, stirring occasionally, until it is just tender. Drain, rinse under cold water, drain well again, and return to the pot.

2. Steam the green beans over boiling water until just tender, about 7 minutes. Run the beans under cold water to stop the cooking process and retain the color; drain well. Set aside.

3. In a small bowl, combine the vinegar, lemon juice, shallot, mustard, salt, sugar, and pepper to taste. Whisk in the oil to blend well. Pour half of the dressing over the pasta. Add the cannellini beans, parsley, and scallions and toss gently to combine. Taste and adjust the seasonings if needed.

4. Arrange the salad greens in the bottom of a large shallow bowl. Top with the pasta and bean mixture. Arrange the green beans, tomatoes, black olives, and artichoke hearts in separate groups on top of the pasta. Drizzle with the remaining dressing, and serve immediately.

SERVES 4

black bean and avocado rice salad

Gluten-free | Soy-free

THIS SALAD IS BEST MADE with cold cooked rice, so keep it in mind for the next time you have leftover rice. This is a hearty and flavorful salad that makes a satisfying meal. If you're assembling it ahead of when you will be serving it, don't cut the avocados until you're ready to serve—otherwise they may turn brown.

2 tablespoons freshly squeezed orange juice

2 tablespoons freshly squeezed lime juice

1 teaspoon grated lime zest

1 tablespoon cider vinegar

1 tablespoon agave nectar

1 garlic clove, minced

½ teaspoon chili powder

½ teaspoon salt

⅛ teaspoon cayenne pepper

2 tablespoons olive oil

3 cups cold cooked rice

1½ cups cooked black beans or 1 (15.5-ounce) can black beans, rinsed and drained

3 tablespoons chopped red onion or scallions

12 cherry tomatoes, halved lengthwise

1 jalapeño chile, seeded and minced (optional)

2 ripe Hass avocados, pitted, peeled, and diced

Torn romaine lettuce leaves, for serving

1. In a small bowl, whisk together the orange juice, lime juice, lime zest, vinegar, agave, garlic, chili powder, salt, and cayenne. Whisk in the oil until well blended.

2. In a large bowl, combine the rice, beans, onion, tomatoes, and jalapeño (if using). Add the avocado to the bowl. Pour on the dressing and toss gently to combine. Taste and adjust the seasonings if needed.

3. Arrange the lettuce on plates, top with the rice and bean mixture, and serve.

SERVES 4

quinoa salad with zucchini and white beans

I LOVE THE WAY the creamy avocado and cannellini beans play against the juicy tomatoes and briny olives in this flavorful salad. Cooked brown rice may be substituted for the quinoa.

1½ cups water

Salt

1 cup uncooked quinoa, rinsed and drained

1 medium-size zucchini, cut into ¼-inch dice

1 small shallot, quartered

2 tablespoons rice vinegar

1 tablespoon freshly squeezed lemon juice

1 tablespoon agave nectar

3 tablespoons olive oil

Freshly ground black pepper

1½ cups cooked cannellini beans
   or 1 (15.5-ounce) can cannellini beans, rinsed and drained

1 ripe Hass avocado, pitted, peeled, and diced

8 cherry or grape tomatoes, halved lengthwise

8 kalamata olives, pitted and halved

2 tablespoons chopped fresh basil

1. Place the water in a saucepan, add ½ teaspoon salt, and bring to a boil. Add the quinoa, return to a boil, then reduce the heat to a simmer. Cover and cook until the quinoa is tender and the water is absorbed, about 15 minutes. About 4 minutes before the quinoa is done cooking, stir in the zucchini. Remove from the heat and let sit for 5 minutes, then transfer the cooked quinoa and zucchini to a bowl and let cool.

2. In a high-speed blender or food processor, combine the shallot, vinegar, lemon juice, and agave and process until smooth. Add the oil and salt and pepper to taste. Process the dressing until well blended.

3. Add the beans, avocado, tomatoes, olives, and basil to the bowl containing the quinoa and zucchini. Pour the dressing over the salad and toss gently to combine. Serve immediately.

SERVES 4

mediterranean rice and chickpea salad

GARLIC, FRESH HERBS, and roasted red peppers imbue this salad with full-bodied Mediterranean flavors. Grated fennel adds a slightly sweet taste and a fresh-tasting crunch, but if fennel is unavailable, you can add some minced celery instead. To save time, you may use a 4-ounce jar of roasted red peppers instead of roasting fresh ones. For another variation, make this salad with cooked quinoa or pasta, or use cannellini beans instead of chickpeas.

2 red bell peppers

1½ tablespoons white wine vinegar

1½ tablespoons freshly squeezed lemon juice

½ teaspoon natural sugar

2 garlic cloves, minced

1 tablespoon minced fresh basil or 1 teaspoon dried basil

½ teaspoon minced fresh oregano or ¼ teaspoon dried oregano

½ teaspoon salt

⅛ teaspoon freshly ground black pepper

3 tablespoons olive oil

2½ cups cold cooked rice

½ cup grated fresh fennel or minced celery

½ small red onion, minced

1½ cups cooked chickpeas or 1 (15.5-ounce) can chickpeas, rinsed and drained

⅓ cup kalamata olives, pitted

Torn mixed salad greens, for serving

1. Preheat the broiler. Halve and seed the bell peppers and place on a baking sheet, skin side up. Broil until the skins are blackened. Place the peppers in a plastic or paper bag and let stand for about 10 minutes. Remove the charred skin from the peppers and discard; cut the peppers into thin strips.

2. In a small bowl, whisk together the vinegar, lemon juice, sugar, garlic, basil, oregano, salt, and pepper. Whisk in the oil in a slow, steady stream until emulsified and smooth.

3. In a large bowl, combine the rice, fennel, onion, chickpeas, olives, and roasted red peppers. Add the dressing and toss well to combine. Taste and adjust the seasonings if needed.

4. Arrange the salad greens on plates, top with the rice mixture, and serve.

SERVES 4

quinoa-avocado salad with pinto beans and salsa

Gluten-free | Soy-free

WITH BOTTLED SALSA and canned pinto beans, this south-of-the-border salad can be put together in minutes.

1½ cups water

Salt

1 cup uncooked quinoa, rinsed and drained

1½ cups cooked pinto beans or 1 (15.5-ounce) can pinto beans, rinsed and drained

1 cup tomato salsa

2 ripe Hass avocados, pitted, peeled, and cut into ½-inch dice

3 tablespoons minced fresh cilantro

2 scallions, minced

Juice and zest of 1 lime

Freshly ground black pepper

Torn mixed salad greens, for serving

1. Place the water in a saucepan, add ½ teaspoon salt, and bring to a boil. Add the quinoa, return to a boil, then reduce the heat to a simmer. Cover and cook until the quinoa is tender and the water is absorbed, about 15 minutes. Remove from the heat and let sit for 5 minutes, then transfer to a large bowl to cool.

2. Add the beans and salsa to the bowl, and toss to combine. Add the avocados, cilantro, scallions, lime juice and zest, and salt and pepper to taste. Toss gently to combine. Taste and adjust the seasonings if needed.

3. Arrange the salad greens on plates, top with the quinoa-bean mixture, and serve.

SERVES 4

quinoa and white bean salad with watercress and tomatoes

SWEET, RIPE TOMATOES COMBINE with creamy white beans and refreshing, crisp watercress for a lovely salad combination that tastes as good as it looks.

1½ cups water

Salt

1 cup uncooked quinoa, rinsed and drained

1 small shallot, quartered

1 garlic clove, crushed

2 tablespoons freshly squeezed lemon juice

1 teaspoon Dijon mustard

3 tablespoons olive oil

Freshly ground black pepper

1½ cups cooked cannellini or other white beans or 1 (15.5-ounce) can cannellini or other white beans, rinsed and drained

8 ounces watercress, thick stems removed, coarsely chopped

16 cherry or grape tomatoes, halved

16 kalamata or brine-cured black olives, pitted and halved

2 tablespoons chopped fresh basil

1. Place the water in a saucepan, add ½ teaspoon salt, and bring to a boil. Add the quinoa, return to a boil, then reduce the heat to a simmer. Cover and cook until the quinoa is tender and the water is absorbed, about 15 minutes. Remove from the heat and let sit for 5 minutes, then transfer to a large bowl and let cool.

2. In a food processor, combine the shallot and garlic and process to a paste. Add the lemon juice, mustard, olive oil, and salt and pepper to taste. Process until well blended, and set aside.

3. Add the beans, watercress, tomatoes, olives, and basil to the bowl containing the quinoa. Pour the dressing over the salad and toss gently to combine. Taste and adjust the seasonings if needed. Serve immediately.

SERVES 4

waldorf rice and spinach salad

Gluten-free | Soy-free option

THE SURPRISING CRUNCH of apples and walnuts in this vibrant, luscious dish inspired by the classic Waldorf salad will make it a favorite addition to the buffet table. Fragrant basmati rice lends an extra touch of sweetness. For soy-free, use a soy-free vegan mayonnaise.

1 large Gala or Fuji apple, peeled (if desired), cored, and cut into ½-inch dice

2 tablespoons freshly squeezed lemon juice

3 cups cold cooked brown basmati rice

¾ cup raisins

1 large rib celery, finely chopped

½ cup chopped toasted walnuts

3 scallions, minced

½ cup vegan mayonnaise

1 teaspoon Dijon mustard

2 tablespoons apple cider vinegar

2 tablespoons apple juice

½ teaspoon natural sugar

½ teaspoon salt

¼ teaspoon ground black pepper

Baby spinach leaves, for serving

1. Place the apple and lemon juice in a large bowl and toss to coat. Add the rice, raisins, celery, walnuts, and scallions.

2. In a small bowl, whisk together the mayonnaise, mustard, vinegar, apple juice, sugar, salt, and pepper until smooth. Add the dressing to the salad and mix gently to combine. Taste and adjust the seasonings if needed.

3. Arrange the spinach leaves in a serving bowl, top with the apple-rice mixture, and serve.

SERVES 4

spicy soba salad with edamame and cucumber

SOBA CAN BE TRICKY to cook because it boils up and over the pot in a big hurry. To solve this, when the water begins to boil, pour a cup of cold water into the pot. Bring it to a boil again, then pour in another cup of cold water. Repeat 4 or 5 times. This will keep the water from boiling over and also helps the noodles cook perfectly.

10 ounces uncooked soba noodles

2 tablespoons dark sesame oil

1 cucumber, peeled, seeded, halved lengthwise, and cut crosswise into ¼-inch slices

3 scallions, minced

1½ cups cooked shelled edamame

2 tablespoons wheat-free tamari

2 tablespoons rice vinegar

1 tablespoon sweet Asian chili sauce

1 to 2 teaspoons sriracha or other spicy Asian chili sauce

1 to 2 teaspoons agave nectar

2 teaspoons toasted sesame seeds

Salt and freshly ground black pepper

1. Cook the soba noodles in a large pot of boiling water, stirring occasionally, until just tender (see headnote). Drain and rinse well under cold water, then transfer the noodles to a large bowl. Add the sesame oil and toss to combine. Add the cucumbers, scallions, and edamame to the noodles.

2. In a small bowl, combine the tamari, vinegar, chili sauce, sriracha, and agave. Mix well, then pour the dressing over the noodle salad, season to taste with salt and pepper, and toss gently to combine. Taste and adjust the seasonings if needed. Sprinkle with the sesame seeds and serve.

SERVES 4

scattered sushi salad

Gluten-free

IN JAPANESE CUISINE THERE are refreshing rice salads called *chirashi-zushi* and *bara-zushi*, which translate as "scattered sushi." My version of a sushi rice salad calls for the traditional Japanese-style glutinous rice, but any kind of cooked rice may be used instead. It's recommended that you soak glutinous rice in cool water for about 30 minutes before using.

1¼ cups uncooked glutinous or sticky rice, soaked and drained

4½ cups water

½ teaspoon salt

2 tablespoons rice vinegar

1 teaspoon natural sugar

2 tablespoons wheat-free tamari

2 teaspoons mellow white miso paste

1 teaspoon mirin (optional)

1 cup shiitake mushrooms, stemmed and thinly sliced

1 medium-size carrot, peeled and cut into 2-inch pieces, then cut lengthwise into thin strips

1 cup snow peas, trimmed and cut diagonally into 1-inch pieces

1 cup cooked shelled edamame

1 cup fresh bean sprouts

1 or 2 scallions, chopped

1 teaspoon dark sesame oil

1 tablespoon toasted sesame seeds

1 sheet nori, cut into 2 x ¼-inch strips

1. Place the rice, 3½ cups of the water, and the salt in a covered saucepan and bring to a boil. Reduce the heat to a low simmer and cook, covered, for 15 minutes. Remove from the heat and set aside for 5 minutes to make sure all of the water is absorbed, then transfer the rice to a shallow bowl and let cool at room temperature.

2. In a small saucepan, heat the rice vinegar with the sugar, stirring to dissolve the sugar. Drizzle the vinegar mixture over the cooled rice.

3. Combine the remaining 1 cup water, tamari, miso paste, and mirin (if using) in a saucepan over medium heat, stirring to dissolve the miso. When the water is simmering, add the mushrooms and carrots and cook until softened, about 2 minutes. Add the snow peas, edamame, and bean sprouts, and cook until the snow peas turn bright green, about 1 minute longer. Remove from the heat. Drain the vegetables, then return them to the saucepan. Add the scallions and sesame oil to the vegetables and toss to coat.

4. Transfer the cooked rice to a large shallow serving bowl or individual bowls and top with the vegetables. Sprinkle with the sesame seeds and nori. Serve at room temperature.

SERVES 4

chickpea tabbouleh

THIS CLASSIC MIDDLE EASTERN SALAD is made with bulgur, tomato, and loads of fresh parsley and mint.

1 ½ cups water

1 cup medium-grind bulgur

Salt

½ small red onion or 3 scallions, minced

1 ½ cups cooked chickpeas or 1 (15.5-ounce) can chickpeas, rinsed and drained

2 medium-size tomatoes, chopped, or 1 ½ cups cherry tomatoes, halved

½ cucumber, peeled, seeded, and chopped

1 cup chopped fresh Italian parsley

¼ cup chopped fresh mint

3 tablespoons olive oil

2 tablespoons freshly squeezed lemon juice

Freshly ground black pepper

1. Bring the water to a boil in a saucepan. Add the bulgur and salt to taste. Remove from the heat, cover, and set aside for 10 minutes.

2. Transfer the softened bulgur to a large serving bowl. Add the onion, chickpeas, tomatoes, cucumber, parsley, and mint.

3. In a small bowl, whisk together the olive oil, lemon juice, and salt and pepper to taste until blended. Pour the dressing over the salad and toss well to combine. Cover and refrigerate for at least 1 hour before serving. Serve chilled.

SERVES 4

lebanese bread salad
with chickpeas

THE LEBANESE HAVE A DELICIOUS bread salad that's similar to Italian panzanella. It's called *fattoush*, and they make it with stale pita bread. I use whole-wheat pita for added flavor and nutrition. The addition of chickpeas and tahini is a departure from the traditional version, but they add lots of protein, turning this refreshing salad into a one-dish meal.

2 garlic cloves, mashed to a paste

2 teaspoons tahini

⅓ cup freshly squeezed lemon juice

¼ cup olive oil

½ teaspoon salt

Pinch of cayenne pepper

2 large or 4 small whole-wheat pita bread rounds

1 large cucumber, peeled, seeded, and chopped

1 large tomato, chopped

½ small red or yellow bell pepper, seeded and chopped

1 small red onion, minced

1½ cups cooked chickpeas or 1 (15.5-ounce) can chickpeas, rinsed and drained

⅓ cup chopped fresh Italian parsley

⅓ cup chopped fresh mint

2 cups shredded romaine lettuce

1. Preheat the oven to 350°F. In a small bowl, whisk together the garlic, tahini, lemon juice, olive oil, salt, and cayenne until blended. Set aside.

2. Place the pitas on a baking sheet and bake until lightly toasted, turning once, about 10 minutes total. Remove from the oven, cut or tear into bite-size pieces, and place in a large bowl. Add the cucumber, tomato, bell pepper, onion, chickpeas, parsley, mint, and as much of the dressing as needed to coat. Toss well to combine, then let sit for 10 to 15 minutes to let the flavors develop.

3. When ready to serve, add the romaine and toss to combine.

SERVES 4

wild about rice salad

THIS SALAD IS A GREAT WAY to use up leftover wild rice, but we enjoy it so much that I usually keep cooked wild rice in the freezer so I can put it together on a whim. If you don't have wild rice on hand, you can use all brown rice or a combination of rice and quinoa. Vary the types of beans and vegetables according to your own preference and availability. Leftover cooked vegetables also make welcome additions. Serve as is or on a bed of lightly dressed salad greens.

2 cups cold cooked long-grain brown rice

1 cup cold cooked wild rice

2 tablespoons cider vinegar

2 tablespoons freshly squeezed lemon juice

1 to 2 teaspoons agave nectar

¾ teaspoon salt

⅛ teaspoon freshly ground black pepper

¼ cup olive oil

1½ cups cooked black or white beans
or 1 (15.5-ounce) can black or white beans,
rinsed and drained

1 celery rib, minced

1 carrot, peeled and shredded

½ red bell pepper, chopped

½ cup fresh or thawed frozen peas

3 scallions, minced

1 (6-ounce) jar marinated artichoke hearts,
drained and coarsely chopped

⅓ cup reconstituted or oil-packed sun-dried
tomatoes, cut into thin strips

¼ cup chopped fresh Italian parsley, dill,
or basil

1. Combine the brown rice and wild rice in a large bowl and set aside.

2. In a small bowl, whisk together the vinegar, lemon juice, agave, salt, and pepper. Add the oil in a steady stream, whisking until emulsified and smooth. Pour the dressing over the rice and toss to coat. Add the beans, celery, carrot, bell pepper, peas, scallions, artichoke hearts, tomatoes, and parsley and toss gently to combine. Taste and adjust the seasonings if needed, and serve at room temperature.

SERVES 4 TO 6

lime-dressed vermicelli with edamame and green papaya

LONG, THIN SHREDS OF PAPAYA and carrot look best in this refreshing salad. Make them yourself with a mandoline slicer or look for pre-shredded vegetables in the produce section of well-stocked Asian markets. Those with milder taste preferences may cut down on or eliminate the red pepper flakes. Spicy food lovers might prefer substituting fresh minced Thai bird's-eye chiles for a jolt of extra-fiery heat.

8 ounces uncooked rice vermicelli

¼ cup dark sesame oil

Juice and zest of 1 lime

2 garlic cloves, minced

2 tablespoons rice wine vinegar

2 teaspoons grated fresh ginger

1 teaspoon natural sugar

¼ teaspoon red pepper flakes, or more as needed

Salt

1 green papaya, peeled and shredded

1 carrot, peeled and shredded

1½ cups cooked shelled edamame

4 scallions, minced

½ cup crushed unsalted roasted peanuts

1. Soak the vermicelli in a bowl of warm water to soften, about 10 minutes. Drain, rinse under cold water, and drain again, then transfer to a large serving bowl. Add 1 tablespoon of the sesame oil, toss to combine, and set aside.

2. In a small bowl, combine the remaining 3 tablespoons sesame oil with the lime juice and zest, garlic, vinegar, ginger, sugar, red pepper flakes, and salt to taste.

3. Add the papaya, carrot, edamame, and scallions to the noodles. Pour on the reserved dressing and toss to combine. Sprinkle with the peanuts and serve.

SERVES 4

citrus-dressed quinoa and black bean salad

THE DAZZLING COMBINATION OF COLORS, textures, and flavors makes this salad an ideal choice for a potluck or company fare. The salad affords a lot of versatility, too—you can easily swap in different vegetables or beans, use rice instead of quinoa, and choose whichever fresh herb you prefer.

1½ cups water

1 teaspoon salt

1 cup uncooked quinoa, rinsed and drained

¼ teaspoon ground turmeric

2 cups small cauliflower florets

Juice and zest of 1 orange

2 tablespoons freshly squeezed lemon juice

2 teaspoons agave nectar

¼ teaspoon freshly ground black pepper

3 tablespoons olive oil

1 carrot, peeled and shredded

1 yellow bell pepper, seeded and cut into ½-inch dice

1½ cups cooked black beans or 1 (15.5-ounce) can black beans, rinsed and drained

3 scallions, minced

1 cup yellow or red grape tomatoes, halved lengthwise

¼ cup chopped fresh Italian parsley, cilantro, basil, or mint

¼ cup sunflower seeds

1. Place the water in a saucepan, add ½ teaspoon of the salt, and bring to a boil. Add the quinoa, return to a boil, then reduce the heat to a simmer. Add the turmeric, cover, and cook until the quinoa is tender and the water is absorbed, about 15 minutes. About 3 minutes before the quinoa is done cooking, stir in the cauliflower. Remove from the heat and let sit for 5 minutes, then transfer the quinoa and cauliflower to a large bowl to cool.

2. In a small bowl, combine the orange juice and zest, lemon juice, agave, the remaining ½ teaspoon salt, and the pepper. Whisk in the oil until blended, then pour the dressing over the quinoa. Add the carrot, bell pepper, black beans, scallions, tomatoes, and parsley and toss to combine. Sprinkle on the sunflower seeds, and serve.

SERVES 4

three-bean rice salad

FOR A VARIATION, SUBSTITUTE CHICKPEAS or white beans for either the kidney or black beans. Diced avocado makes a good addition. Roasted red bell pepper may be substituted for the pimiento.

6 ounces green beans, trimmed and cut into 1-inch pieces (about 2 cups)

1½ cups cooked dark red kidney beans or 1 (15.5-ounce) can dark red kidney beans, rinsed and drained

1½ cups cooked black beans or 1 (15.5-ounce) can black beans, rinsed and drained

1 cucumber, peeled, seeded, and chopped

1 (2-ounce) jar chopped pimientos, drained

2 tablespoons minced fresh Italian parsley

3 tablespoons freshly squeezed lemon juice

1 garlic clove, minced

½ teaspoon dry mustard

¾ teaspoon salt

¼ teaspoon freshly ground black pepper

3 tablespoons olive oil

3 cups cold cooked long-grain brown rice

2 scallions, minced

Torn mixed salad greens, for serving

8 cherry or grape tomatoes, halved lengthwise

1. Steam the green beans over boiling water until tender, about 7 minutes. Run the beans under cold water to stop the cooking process and retain the color; drain well.

2. In a large bowl, combine the green beans, kidney beans, black beans, cucumber, pimientos, and parsley. Set aside.

3. In a small bowl, whisk together the lemon juice, garlic, dry mustard, salt, and pepper. Whisk in the oil until emulsified and smooth. Pour the dressing over the bean mixture and toss to coat. Let marinate for 20 minutes.

4. Add the rice and scallions to the bean mixture and toss to combine. Taste and adjust the seasonings if needed. Arrange the salad greens in a serving bowl or on plates, top with the rice-bean mixture and the tomatoes, and serve.

SERVES 6

roasted sweet potato and black bean salad

THIS YUMMY SALAD MAKES a nice change from white potato salad (and is much more nutritious, too). Serving it over lettuce with the addition of black beans makes it a meal. Delicious any time of year, it looks especially lovely on a buffet table during autumn get-togethers.

1½ pounds sweet potatoes, peeled and cut into 1-inch dice

3 tablespoons olive oil, plus more for drizzling

Salt and freshly ground black pepper

1½ cups cooked black beans or 1 (15.5-ounce) can black beans, rinsed and drained

1 cup fresh or thawed frozen peas

⅓ cup unsalted roasted cashews or pecan pieces

¼ cup dried cranberries

1 celery rib, minced

3 scallions, chopped

¼ cup freshly squeezed orange juice

1 tablespoon freshly squeezed lemon juice

1 to 2 teaspoons agave nectar or maple syrup

4 cups chopped romaine lettuce

1. Preheat the oven to 425°F. Lightly oil a baking sheet and spread the sweet potatoes on the sheet in a single layer. Drizzle with a little olive oil. Season to taste with salt and pepper. Roast the sweet potatoes until just tender, about 30 minutes, turning once about halfway through. Set aside to cool.

2. In a large bowl, combine the black beans, peas, cashews, cranberries, celery, and scallions.

3. In a small bowl, combine the orange juice, lemon juice, agave, ⅛ teaspoon freshly ground black pepper, and salt to taste. Whisk in the 3 tablespoons oil to blend.

4. Add the cooled sweet potatoes to the bowl containing the vegetables. Pour the dressing over the salad and toss gently to combine. Taste and adjust the seasonings if needed.

5. Arrange the lettuce leaves in a shallow serving bowl, top with the potato-bean mixture, and serve.

SERVES 4

potato salad with avocado dressing

YOU CAN DEFINITELY HOLD THE MAYO with this fabulous potato salad. The luscious dressing is made with avocado and cucumber, and there are lots of goodies in the salad to keep the potatoes company, from protein-rich cannellini beans to flavorful kalamata olives and sun-dried tomatoes—oh, and more avocado!

1½ pounds Yukon gold or new potatoes, peeled or scrubbed, cut into 1-inch chunks

3 scallions, minced

1 celery rib, minced

½ cup thawed frozen green peas

1½ cups cooked cannellini beans or 1 (15.5-ounce) can cannellini beans, rinsed and drained

⅓ cup kalamata olives, pitted and halved

⅓ cup minced reconstituted or oil-packed sun-dried tomatoes

⅓ cup chopped peeled cucumber

2 garlic cloves, crushed

2 tablespoons freshly squeezed lemon juice

2 ripe Hass avocados, halved, pitted, and peeled

½ cup fresh cilantro or basil

Salt and freshly ground black pepper

1. Place the potatoes in a large saucepan with enough cold water to cover. Bring to a boil, salt the water, then reduce the heat to a simmer and cook until the potatoes are just tender, 12 to 15 minutes. Drain well, transfer to a large bowl, and let cool.

2. Add the scallions, celery, peas, beans, olives, and tomatoes to the bowl with the cooled potatoes.

3. In a food processor, combine the cucumber, garlic, and lemon juice, and process until smooth. Dice half of one avocado and add it to the potato mixture. Add the remaining 3 avocado halves to the food processor, along with ¼ cup of the cilantro and salt and pepper to taste, and process until smooth and creamy. Taste and adjust the seasonings if needed. Add the dressing to the potato mixture, along with the remaining ¼ cup cilantro, and toss gently to combine. Serve immediately.

SERVES 4

cumin-spiced quinoa salad
with jalapeño pesto

THIS LIVELY SALAD GETS ITS PUNCH from a bold jalapeño pesto that coats the quinoa, pinto beans, and vegetables with its vibrant flavor.

2 tablespoons olive oil

1½ teaspoons ground cumin

1¾ cups water, plus more for pesto

Salt

1¼ cups uncooked quinoa, rinsed and drained

½ small red onion, minced

1½ cups cooked pinto beans or 1 (15.5-ounce) can pinto beans, rinsed and drained

2 jalapeño chiles, halved and seeded

1 large garlic clove, crushed

½ cup chopped fresh Italian parsley or cilantro

2 tablespoons freshly squeezed lime juice

½ teaspoon natural sugar

½ teaspoon chili powder

1 ripe Hass avocado, pitted, peeled, and diced

8 cherry or grape tomatoes, halved lengthwise

Torn mixed salad greens, for serving

1. Heat the oil in a small skillet over medium heat. Add the cumin and stir until fragrant, about 30 seconds. Set aside.

2. Place the water in a saucepan, add ½ teaspoon salt, and bring to a boil. Add the quinoa, return to a boil, then reduce the heat to a simmer. Cover and cook until the quinoa is tender and the water is absorbed, about 15 minutes. Remove from the heat and let sit for 5 minutes, then transfer to a large bowl. Add the cumin-oil mixture to the quinoa, along with the onion and 1 cup of the pinto beans. Toss to combine, then set aside to cool.

3. In a food processor, pulse the jalapeños and garlic until minced. Add the parsley, lime juice, sugar, chili powder, remaining ½ cup pinto beans, and salt to taste. Process until smooth, adding about 2 tablespoons of water to make a smooth paste.

4. Add the jalapeño pesto to the quinoa mixture, along with the avocado and tomatoes, and toss to coat. Taste and adjust the seasonings if needed.

5. Arrange the salad greens on plates, top with the quinoa mixture, and serve.

SERVES 4

quinoa and black bean salad

Gluten-free | Soy-free

A TOUCH OF MUSTARD and smoked paprika enlivens the dressing in this hearty salad made with black beans, quinoa, and a variety of vegetables. Toasted walnuts add crunch, and a bed of chiffonade-cut romaine lettuce provides a refreshing base.

1½ cups water

1 teaspoon salt

1 cup uncooked quinoa, rinsed and drained

2 tablespoons freshly squeezed lemon juice

1 tablespoon rice vinegar

1 tablespoon olive oil

1 teaspoon agave nectar

1 teaspoon Dijon mustard

⅛ teaspoon dried oregano

⅛ teaspoon smoked paprika

¼ teaspoon freshly ground black pepper

3 scallions, chopped

1 large carrot, peeled and shredded

1½ cups cooked black beans or 1 (15.5-ounce) can black beans, rinsed and drained

1 large tomato, diced

½ cup kalamata olives, chopped

¼ cup chopped fresh Italian parsley, basil, or cilantro

½ cup toasted walnut pieces

1 small head romaine lettuce, cut into ⅛-inch chiffonade

1. Place the water in a saucepan, add ½ teaspoon of the salt, and bring to a boil. Add the quinoa, return to a boil, then reduce the heat to a simmer. Cover and cook until the quinoa is tender and the water is absorbed, about 15 minutes. Remove from the heat and let sit for 5 minutes, then transfer to a large bowl to cool.

2. In a large bowl, combine the lemon juice, vinegar, oil, agave, mustard, oregano, paprika, the remaining ½ teaspoon of salt, and pepper. Mix well. Add the scallions, carrot, black beans, tomato, olives, and parsley. Add the cooled quinoa and the walnuts and toss to coat. Taste and adjust the seasonings if needed.

3. Arrange the romaine on plates, top with the quinoa-bean mixture, and serve.

SERVES 4

stovetop simmers and stews

hoppin' john with kale

THE TRADITIONAL SOUTHERN DISH becomes a nourishing one-pot meal with the addition of kale. For a variation, any other dark leafy greens may be used in place of the kale. For a soy-free option, use soy-free vegan sour cream.

1 tablespoon olive oil or ¼ cup water

1 medium-size yellow onion, chopped

1 cup uncooked long-grain brown rice

1 teaspoon dried thyme

½ teaspoon red pepper flakes (optional)

1 teaspoon salt

⅛ teaspoon freshly ground black pepper

2½ to 3 cups vegetable broth

12 ounces kale, thick stems removed, coarsely chopped

1½ cups cooked black-eyed peas or 1 (15.5-ounce) can black-eyed peas, rinsed and drained

1 teaspoon liquid smoke

Vegan sour cream, purchased or homemade (page 101), for serving

Tabasco sauce, for serving

1. Heat the oil or water in a large pot over medium heat. Add the onion and cook for 5 minutes to soften. Add the rice, thyme, red pepper flakes (if using), salt, and pepper. Stir in 2½ cups of the broth and bring to a boil, then reduce the heat to a simmer, cover, and cook for 35 minutes.

2. Add the kale a little at a time, stirring to wilt. Add the black-eyed peas and the remaining ½ cup broth, if needed. Cook, uncovered, until the rice and kale are tender, about 10 minutes longer. Stir in the liquid smoke, then taste and adjust the seasonings if needed. Serve hot, with sour cream and Tabasco alongside.

SERVES 4

arroz con tempeh

THE FIRM, MEATY TEXTURE of tempeh is ideal in this vegan version of the Spanish classic arroz con pollo. If you're not a fan of tempeh or want to go soy-free, this is also good made with either seitan or red beans.

1 tablespoon olive oil or ¼ cup water

1 medium-size onion, chopped

1 red bell pepper, seeded and chopped

2 garlic cloves, chopped

8 ounces tempeh, steamed and cut into 1-inch pieces (see page 6)

½ teaspoon dried oregano

½ teaspoon ground cumin

¼ teaspoon saffron threads or ground turmeric

1 cup uncooked long-grain brown rice

1 (14.5-ounce) can diced tomatoes, undrained

2½ cups vegetable broth

8 ounces green beans, trimmed and cut into 1-inch pieces (about 2 cups)

Salt

½ cup fresh or thawed frozen peas

¼ cup coarsely chopped pimiento-stuffed green olives

⅓ cup tomato salsa

Freshly ground black pepper

1. Heat the oil or water in a large saucepan over medium heat. Add the onion and bell pepper and cook until the vegetables are softened, about 5 minutes. Add the garlic, tempeh, oregano, cumin, and saffron and sauté for 1 to 2 minutes longer. Stir in the rice, then add the tomatoes with their juices, broth, green beans, and salt to taste. Cover and simmer until the rice is tender, about 35 minutes.

2. Add the peas, olives, and salsa, season to taste with pepper, and cook until heated through, about 5 minutes. Taste and adjust the seasonings if needed. Serve hot.

SERVES 4

rice and broccoli with lemony white bean sauce

THE CREAMY LEMONY SAUCE imbues rice and broccoli with a luscious flavor and amps up the protein because it's made with white beans. To bulk up the dish, you may add additional cooked beans (left whole) to the rice and vegetable mixture before adding the sauce.

1 tablespoon olive oil or ¼ cup water

1 medium-size yellow onion, minced

2 garlic cloves, minced

1½ teaspoons dried basil

1 cup uncooked long-grain brown rice

2½ cups hot vegetable broth

3 cups small broccoli florets

1½ cups cooked Great Northern or other white beans or 1 (15.5-ounce) can Great Northern or other white beans, rinsed and drained

2 tablespoons freshly squeezed lemon juice

Salt and freshly ground black pepper

2 tablespoons chopped fresh Italian parsley

1. In a large saucepan, heat the oil or water over medium heat. Add the onion, garlic, and 1 teaspoon of the basil and cook until the onion is softened, about 5 minutes. Stir in the rice and 2 cups of the broth and bring to a boil. Reduce the heat to a simmer, cover, and cook until the rice is almost tender, 35 to 40 minutes.

2. Add the broccoli and continue to cook until the rice and broccoli are tender, about 5 minutes.

3. While the rice is cooking, combine the beans, the remaining ½ cup broth, the lemon juice, and the remaining ½ teaspoon basil in a high-speed blender or food processor and puree until smooth. Season to taste with salt and pepper.

4. Transfer the rice and broccoli to a large bowl, top with the sauce, sprinkle the parsley over all, and serve.

SERVES 4

japanese vegetable curry

MILDER AND THICKER THAN OTHER CURRIES and slightly sweet, Japanese curries are typically thickened with a roux. This version cuts the fat and adds flavor by pureeing some of the vegetables in the curry to thicken it. This is also good made with fresh or frozen shelled edamame instead of the tofu, and snow peas instead of the green peas. S&B brand curry powder works best in this dish.

1 tablespoon vegetable oil or ¼ cup water

1 large yellow onion, chopped

2 carrots, peeled and cut into ¼-inch-thick slices

1½ to 2 tablespoons yellow curry powder

1½ tablespoons tomato paste

1 tablespoon wheat-free tamari

1 to 2 teaspoons agave nectar

¼ teaspoon cayenne pepper (optional)

⅓ cup applesauce

3 cups vegetable broth

1 large russet potato, peeled and cut into 1-inch dice

Salt and freshly ground black pepper

1 tablespoon mellow miso paste

8 ounces extra-firm tofu, well drained, blotted dry, and diced

¾ cup fresh or thawed frozen peas

1. Heat the oil or water in a large pot over medium heat. Add the onion and cook until softened, about 5 minutes. Add the carrots, then stir in the curry powder, tomato paste, tamari, agave, cayenne (if using), applesauce, and broth and bring to a boil. Reduce the heat to a simmer and add the potato and salt and pepper to taste. Simmer until the vegetables are tender, about 30 minutes.

2. Transfer about 2 cups of the mixture to a high-speed blender or food processor. Add the miso paste, and puree until smooth. Stir the vegetable puree back into the curry along with the tofu and peas, and simmer for 5 minutes longer. Taste and adjust the seasonings if needed. Serve hot.

SERVES 4

vegetable étouffée

Soy-free

THERE ARE MANY VARIATIONS on the classic Cajun stew called *étouffée*, which translates from the French as "smothered" and is usually made with crawfish or shrimp. This brimming-with-vegetables version still has that great New Orleans taste because it's based on a dark roux, the traditional butter-and-flour thickener (although olive oil stands in for butter here), and the famous Cajun "trinity" of onion, celery, and bell pepper. The ingredient list may seem long, but this stew cooks in only 30 minutes. Traditionally, this is a "serve over rice" dish.

3 tablespoons all-purpose flour

1 tablespoon olive oil

1 medium-size yellow onion, finely chopped

1 celery rib, finely chopped

1 green bell pepper, seeded and finely chopped

2 medium-size zucchini, halved lengthwise and cut into ½-inch slices

4 garlic cloves, minced

2 cups vegetable broth

1½ cups cooked dark red kidney beans or 1 (15.5-ounce) can dark red kidney beans, rinsed and drained

1 (14.5-ounce) can crushed tomatoes

3 scallions, chopped

1 teaspoon dried thyme

½ teaspoon filé powder

1 bay leaf

¼ teaspoon cayenne pepper

Salt and freshly ground black pepper

2 tablespoons minced fresh Italian parsley

Hot pepper sauce (optional)

Cooked brown rice, for serving

1. Heat a large skillet over medium heat. Add the flour and stir constantly until it turns light brown, 3 to 5 minutes; watch carefully so it does not burn. Transfer the flour to a small plate and set aside.

2. Heat the oil in the same skillet over medium heat. Add the onion, celery, bell pepper, zucchini, and garlic, cover, and cook until soft, about 10 minutes. Add the browned flour, stirring to coat the vegetables. Add the broth, beans, tomatoes, scallions, thyme, filé powder, bay leaf, cayenne, and salt and pepper to taste. Bring to a boil, then reduce the heat to a simmer and cook, stirring, until thickened, 10 to 15 minutes.

3. Add the parsley, then taste and adjust the seasoning, adding a splash of hot pepper sauce if desired. Serve hot over rice.

SERVES 4

black bean and two-tomato stew with quinoa

THE COMBINATION OF FIRE-ROASTED and sun-dried tomatoes adds a richness of flavor to this wholesome and delicious stew made with whole grains, beans, and lots of veggies.

1 tablespoon olive oil or ¼ cup water

1 large yellow onion, chopped

1 red bell pepper, seeded and chopped

2 garlic cloves, minced

1 jalapeño chile, seeded and minced

1 cup uncooked quinoa, rinsed and drained

1 (14.5-ounce) can fire-roasted diced tomatoes, undrained

1 teaspoon dried marjoram

1 teaspoon salt

¼ teaspoon freshly ground black pepper

3 cups vegetable broth, plus more if needed

1½ cups cooked black beans or 1 (15.5-ounce) black beans, rinsed and drained

1 or 2 scallions, minced

2 tablespoons chopped sun-dried tomatoes

2 tablespoons minced fresh Italian parsley or cilantro

Hot pepper sauce, for serving (optional)

1. Heat the oil or water in a large pot over medium heat. Add the onion, bell pepper, garlic, and jalapeño. Cook for 5 minutes to soften. Stir in the quinoa, tomatoes with their juices, marjoram, salt, pepper, and broth and bring to a boil. Reduce the heat to a simmer, cover, and cook, stirring occasionally, until the vegetables and quinoa are tender, 20 to 25 minutes. If the mixture becomes too dry, add a small amount of additional broth.

2. Stir the beans, scallions, sun-dried tomatoes, and parsley into the pot. Cover and remove from the heat. Set aside for 5 minutes to allow the flavors to blend. Serve hot with hot pepper sauce, if desired.

SERVES 4

risotto primavera

RED PEPPER, CARROTS, AND ZUCCHINI add color, texture, and flavor to this creamy risotto that features protein-rich edamame. Serve it in shallow soup bowls with a crisp salad and warm garlic bread for a satisfying meal.

1 tablespoon olive oil or ¼ cup water

½ red bell pepper, seeded and finely chopped

1 carrot, peeled and grated

1 small zucchini, shredded

2 garlic cloves, minced

1½ cups uncooked Arborio rice

1½ cups shelled fresh or thawed frozen edamame

¼ cup dry white wine

5 cups hot vegetable broth

Salt and freshly ground black pepper

¼ cup chopped fresh Italian parsley or basil

1 tablespoon freshly squeezed lemon juice

1. Heat the oil or water in a large saucepan over medium heat until hot. Add the bell pepper, carrot, zucchini, and garlic and sauté for 5 minutes. Stir in the rice and edamame. Add the wine and simmer gently, stirring occasionally, until it has been absorbed.

2. Add ½ cup of the hot broth and cook, stirring constantly, until all of the liquid has been absorbed. Adjust the heat as necessary to maintain a simmer. Continue cooking, adding broth ½ cup at a time and stirring until it is absorbed, until the rice is tender but still firm and the risotto is thick and creamy, about 25 minutes (you may not need all of the broth).

3. Add salt and pepper to taste, then add the parsley and lemon juice. Taste and adjust the seasonings if needed. Serve immediately.

SERVES 4

jambalaya

A COMBINATION OF RED BEANS and vegan sausage provides the protein in this vegan jambalaya, made with the culinary "holy trinity" of onion, green bell pepper, and celery and simmered in a spicy tomato broth.

1 tablespoon olive oil

8 ounces vegan sausage links, cut into ½-inch slices

1 medium-size yellow onion, chopped

1 rib celery, chopped

1 green bell pepper, seeded and coarsely chopped

3 garlic cloves, minced

2 tablespoons tomato paste

1 (14.5-ounce) can fire-roasted diced tomatoes, undrained

1½ cups cooked dark red kidney beans or 1 (15.5-ounce can) dark red kidney beans, rinsed and drained

1 cup vegetable broth

½ cup uncooked long-grain brown rice

½ teaspoon dried thyme

½ teaspoon filé powder (optional)

1 tablespoon chopped fresh Italian parsley

½ teaspoon salt

1 teaspoon Tabasco sauce

Heat the oil in a large pot over medium heat. Add the sausage and cook until browned, about 5 minutes. Remove the sausage from the pot and reserve. Return the pot to the heat and add the onion, celery, bell pepper, and garlic. Add a few tablespoons of water or vegetable broth if necessary to prevent the vegetables from sticking. Cook, stirring occasionally, until the vegetables begin to soften, about 5 minutes. Stir in the tomato paste, then add the tomatoes with their juices, beans, broth, rice, thyme, filé powder (if using), parsley, and salt. Cover and simmer until the vegetables and rice are soft, about 20 minutes. A few minutes before serving time, stir in the Tabasco and the sausage. Taste and adjust the seasonings if needed, and serve hot.

SERVES 4

louisiana red beans and rice

THIS IS ALSO KNOWN AS "Monday night supper" in New Orleans, where virtually every kitchen has a spicy pot of kidney beans simmering on the stove come Monday. Filé powder, made from ground sassafras leaves, is used to season and thicken gumbos and other Creole dishes. It is available in specialty food shops and in the gourmet section of well-stocked super-markets. If unavailable, it is okay to omit it.

1 tablespoon olive oil or ¼ cup water

1 medium-size red onion, finely chopped

1 small green bell pepper, seeded and finely chopped

1 celery rib, minced

4 garlic cloves, minced

1 cup uncooked long-grain brown rice

1 (28-ounce) can fire-roasted diced tomatoes, undrained

3 cups cooked dark red kidney beans or 2 (15.5-ounce) cans dark red kidney beans, rinsed and drained

2 cups vegetable broth or water

1 teaspoon dried thyme

½ teaspoon filé powder

½ teaspoon smoked paprika

½ teaspoon salt

¼ teaspoon cayenne pepper

Tabasco sauce, for serving

1. Heat the oil or water in a large saucepan over medium heat. Add the onion, bell pepper, celery, and garlic, and cook for 3 to 5 minutes to soften. Stir in the rice, tomatoes with their juices, beans, broth, thyme, filé powder, paprika, salt, and cayenne. Bring to a boil, then reduce the heat to a simmer, cover, and cook until the rice and vegetables are tender, about 35 minutes.

2. Taste and adjust the seasonings if needed. Serve hot, with Tabasco to taste.

SERVES 4

moroccan chickpeas
with couscous

THE APPLE JUICE AND CINNAMON add a spicy sweetness to this exotic-tasting dish. Couscous can be ready in minutes, so if you've made the chickpeas in advance, this can truly be a "fast food" meal. For a gluten-free option, serve over hot cooked quinoa or rice instead of couscous.

1 tablespoon olive oil or ¼ cup water

1 medium-size onion, chopped

1 carrot, peeled and chopped

1 jalapeño chile, seeded and minced

3 garlic cloves, minced

1 teaspoon grated fresh ginger

1 teaspoon dried marjoram

½ teaspoon ground cinnamon

½ teaspoon ground cumin

1 (14.5-ounce) can diced tomatoes, undrained

3 cups cooked chickpeas or 2 (15.5-ounce) cans chickpeas, rinsed and drained

1 cup apple juice

1 cup fresh or thawed frozen peas

1 tablespoon freshly squeezed lemon juice

Salt

2 tablespoons toasted slivered almonds or minced scallions

3 to 4 cups hot cooked couscous

1. Heat the oil or water in a large pot over medium heat. Add the onion, carrot, jalapeño, and garlic, cover, and cook until softened, about 5 minutes. Add the ginger, marjoram, cinnamon, and cumin. Stir in the tomatoes with their juices, chickpeas, and apple juice, and simmer, covered, for 20 minutes, stirring occasionally.

2. Add the peas, lemon juice, and salt to taste, and simmer, uncovered, until the desired consistency is reached, about 10 minutes longer. Sprinkle with the almonds, and serve over the couscous.

SERVES 4

french lentils with sweet potatoes and chard

THIS DISH IS EXTREMELY SATISFYING on its own, but for even more flavor and heartiness, add sautéed sliced vegan sausage links just before serving.

1 tablespoon olive oil or ¼ cup water

1 large onion, chopped

3 garlic cloves, minced

¼ teaspoon red pepper flakes

½ teaspoon dried thyme

4 cups vegetable broth

½ cup dry white wine

1 cup dried French green lentils

2 sweet potatoes, peeled and cut into ½-inch dice

1 teaspoon salt

Freshly ground black pepper

8 cups chopped stemmed chard

1. Heat the oil or water in a large pot over medium heat. Add the onion and cook until softened, 5 minutes. Add the garlic, red pepper flakes, and thyme, and cook until fragrant, 30 seconds. Stir in the broth and wine, increase the heat to high, and bring to a boil. Add the lentils, reduce the heat to a simmer, and cook, partially covered, for 20 minutes.

2. Add the sweet potatoes, salt, and pepper to taste and cook for 10 minutes longer. Add the chard and continue to cook, stirring occasionally, until the ingredients are tender, about 10 minutes longer. Serve hot.

SERVES 4

almond bulgur with black beans, tomatoes, and kale

THIS HEARTY DISH MADE WITH BULGUR and black beans has a wholesome stick-to-your-ribs quality. With fresh kale and tomatoes and creamy almond butter, it makes an appealing one-dish meal.

½ cup medium-grind bulgur

1¼ cups hot vegetable broth

1 tablespoon olive oil or ¼ cup water

1 large yellow onion, finely chopped

½ teaspoon smoked paprika

½ teaspoon freshly ground black pepper

½ teaspoon ground coriander

¼ teaspoon ground cumin

⅛ teaspoon ground cinnamon

⅛ teaspoon ground nutmeg or cloves

9 ounces kale, thick stems removed, chopped

4 scallions, chopped

1½ cups cooked black beans or 1 (15.5-ounce) can black beans, rinsed and drained

2 medium-size tomatoes, diced, or 1 (14.5-ounce) can diced tomatoes, drained

2 tablespoons almond butter

2 tablespoons freshly squeezed lemon juice

Salt

¼ cup sliced or slivered toasted almonds

1. Place the bulgur in a bowl. Add the vegetable broth, cover, and set aside for 15 minutes.

2. Heat the oil or water in a large skillet over medium heat. Add the onion and the spices and cook, stirring, until the onion is softened, about 5 minutes. Add the kale, scallions, beans, tomatoes, and the soaked bulgur and any unabsorbed broth. Reduce the heat to low, cover, and simmer until the ingredients are tender and the flavors are well blended, about 10 minutes.

3. In a small bowl, combine the almond butter and lemon juice, stirring to blend, then stir the mixture into the pilaf and season to taste with salt. Sprinkle with the toasted almonds and serve hot.

SERVES 4

indian-spiced risotto

CHICKPEAS, CAULIFLOWER, AND RICE, a favorite Indian combination, are featured in this spicy risotto-type mélange. Other vegetables, such as broccoli or cabbage, may be added or substituted to suit your personal taste.

1 tablespoon vegetable oil or ¼ cup water

1 large onion, thinly sliced

2 garlic cloves, minced

2 teaspoons minced fresh ginger

¾ cup uncooked basmati rice

3 cups small cauliflower florets

1½ cups cooked chickpeas or 1 (15.5-ounce) can chickpeas, rinsed and drained

¾ teaspoon ground coriander

¾ teaspoon ground cumin

¼ teaspoon ground cinnamon or cardamom

¼ teaspoon ground turmeric

½ teaspoon salt

⅛ teaspoon cayenne pepper

1½ cups vegetable broth, plus more if needed

1 (13-ounce) can unsweetened coconut milk, plus more if needed

½ cup fresh or thawed frozen peas

1. Heat the oil or water in a large skillet over medium heat. Add the onion, garlic, and ginger, and cook until the onion is soft and lightly browned, about 7 minutes. Add the rice, cauliflower, chickpeas, and spices. Add the broth and bring to a boil. Reduce the heat to a simmer, stir in the coconut milk, cover, and simmer until the vegetables and rice are tender and the liquid has been absorbed, 30 to 40 minutes. If the mixture is too dry, add a small amount of additional broth or coconut milk.

2. Stir in the peas. Taste and adjust the seasonings if needed. Serve hot.

SERVES 4

succotash pilaf
with grape tomatoes

Gluten-free | Soy-free

THE OLD-FASHIONED VEGETABLE SIDE DISH is transformed into a meal with the addition of brown rice and tomatoes. Instead of the usual lima beans, you may substitute edamame for a fresh update.

2 teaspoons olive oil

4 scallions, minced

½ small red bell pepper, seeded and chopped

½ cup uncooked brown basmati rice

1¼ cups vegetable broth

Salt and freshly ground black pepper

1½ cups frozen baby lima beans

1½ cups fresh or frozen corn kernels

1 cup grape tomatoes, halved

1½ tablespoons minced fresh Italian parsley

1. Heat the oil in a large skillet or saucepan over medium heat. Add the scallions, bell pepper, and rice. Cook, stirring, for 1 minute. Add the broth and bring to a boil. Reduce the heat to a simmer and season to taste with salt and pepper. Cover and cook for 20 minutes.

2. Stir in the lima beans and cook, covered, until the rice and limas are just tender, 10 to 15 minutes. Stir in the corn and cook for 5 minutes longer. Remove from the heat and stir in the tomatoes and parsley. Taste and adjust the seasonings if needed. Serve hot.

SERVES 4

jamaican jerk tempeh and vegetables

THE HEADY INTENSITY of Jamaican jerk spices makes this dish especially flavorful, as the spices are readily absorbed by the tempeh. Serve over rice or couscous, with mango chutney and chopped peanuts as accompaniments.

2 teaspoons natural sugar

1 teaspoon dried thyme

1 teaspoon dried oregano

1 teaspoon ground cumin

1 teaspoon ground allspice or cinnamon

½ teaspoon ground coriander

½ teaspoon cayenne pepper

8 ounces tempeh, steamed and cut into 1-inch pieces (see page 6)

1 tablespoon olive oil

1 tablespoon dark rum (optional)

½ cup vegetable broth

3 garlic cloves

1 medium-size red onion, chopped

1 large sweet potato, peeled and diced

1 medium-size zucchini, halved lengthwise and thinly sliced

1 (28-ounce) can diced tomatoes, undrained

1 tablespoon wheat-free tamari

Salt

1. In a small bowl, combine the sugar, thyme, oregano, cumin, allspice, coriander, and cayenne. Add the tempeh and toss to coat.

2. Heat the oil in a large skillet over medium heat. Add the tempeh pieces (reserving any remaining spice mixture) and cook until lightly browned, about 5 minutes. Add the rum, if using. Remove the tempeh from the skillet and reserve.

3. Without wiping out the skillet, add the broth to the same skillet and heat over medium-high heat. Add the garlic, onion, and sweet potato, cover, and cook until softened, about 10 minutes. Uncover, and stir in the zucchini, tomatoes with their juices, tamari, and salt to taste. Add the reserved tempeh and the remaining spice mixture and stir gently to combine. Bring to a boil, then reduce the heat to a simmer and cook until the vegetables are tender and the flavors are blended, about 30 minutes. Taste and adjust the seasonings if needed. Serve hot.

SERVES 4

quinoa and lentils with butternut squash and rapini

Gluten-free | Soy-free

HEARTY, HEALTHFUL, AND DELICIOUS, this simmer of lentils, quinoa, and squash also includes rapini (aka broccoli rabe) and walnuts for a wide variety of textures and flavors. If rapini is unavailable, substitute 8 ounces of your favorite green vegetable.

1 tablespoon olive oil or ¼ cup water

1 medium-size red onion, minced

3 garlic cloves, minced

¾ cup dried brown or green lentils

4 cups vegetable broth

1 small butternut squash, peeled, seeded, and diced (about 3 cups)

¾ cup uncooked quinoa, rinsed and drained

½ teaspoon dried thyme

½ teaspoon red pepper flakes (optional)

Salt and freshly ground black pepper

8 ounces rapini, thick stems removed, coarsely chopped

¼ cup toasted walnut pieces

1. Heat the oil or water in a large pot over medium heat. Add the onion and garlic and cook for 5 minutes to soften. Stir in the lentils and broth and bring to a boil. Reduce the heat to a simmer and cook for 15 minutes.

2. Add the squash, quinoa, thyme, red pepper flakes (if using), and salt and pepper to taste. Cover and cook for 15 minutes longer.

3. Stir in the rapini and cook on low heat until the ingredients are tender and the flavors are well blended, about 15 minutes longer. Sprinkle with the walnuts and serve hot.

SERVES 4

chickpea and kale stew

THIS RICH-TASTING STEW is well balanced with protein, vegetables, and complex carbs, so no accompaniments are needed, although warm flatbread and a crisp green salad make terrific additions to the table.

1 tablespoon olive oil or ¼ cup water

1 large yellow onion, chopped

3 garlic cloves, minced

2 russet potatoes, peeled and cut into ½-inch dice

2 teaspoons ground coriander

1 teaspoon ground cumin

½ teaspoon dried oregano or marjoram

¼ teaspoon cayenne pepper

2 tablespoons tomato paste

2 cups vegetable broth, plus more if needed

6 cups chopped stemmed kale

1 red or green bell pepper, chopped

1 (14.5-ounce) can diced tomatoes, undrained

3 cups cooked chickpeas or 2 (15.5-ounce) cans chickpeas, rinsed and drained

½ teaspoon salt, or to taste

1. Heat the oil or water in a large pot over medium heat. Add the onion and cook, stirring occasionally, until softened, about 5 minutes. Add the garlic, potatoes, coriander, cumin, oregano, cayenne, and tomato paste and cook, stirring, for 30 seconds. Add the broth and kale and cook, stirring occasionally, to wilt the kale. Stir in the bell pepper, tomatoes with their juices, chickpeas, and salt and simmer until the vegetables are tender, about 20 minutes, adding a little more broth if desired.

2. For a thicker texture, if desired, scoop out about 1 cup of the stew and puree it in a high-speed blender or food processor, then return it to the pot; or use an immersion blender to puree some of the stew right in the pot. Taste and adjust the seasonings if needed. Serve hot.

SERVES 4

provençal vegetables
with israeli couscous

Gluten-free option | Soy-free

I ESPECIALLY LIKE THIS flavorful vegetable mélange over Israeli couscous, but you may serve it over rice or quinoa if you prefer to make it gluten-free.

1 tablespoon olive oil or ¼ cup water

1 small eggplant, peeled and cut into ½-inch cubes

1 medium-size onion, diced

1 red bell pepper, seeded and cut into ½-inch pieces

2 garlic cloves, minced

2 small zucchini, cut into ½-inch cubes

2 medium-size tomatoes, diced, or 1 (14.5-ounce) can diced tomatoes, drained

2 tablespoons chopped fresh Italian parsley

1 tablespoon chopped fresh basil

1 teaspoon minced fresh thyme

1 teaspoon salt

⅛ teaspoon cayenne pepper

3 cups hot cooked Israeli couscous

Heat the oil or water in a large saucepan over medium heat. Add the eggplant and onion, cover, and cook until softened, about 5 minutes. Add the bell pepper and garlic, cover, and cook, stirring occasionally, until soft, about 5 minutes longer. Add the zucchini, tomatoes, parsley, basil, thyme, salt, and cayenne and cook, partially covered, until all of the vegetables are tender, about 20 minutes. Taste and adjust the seasonings if needed. Serve over the couscous.

SERVES 4

vegetable tagine

FRAGRANT WITH HERBS, SPICES, and lemon zest, this flavorful Moroccan stew is traditionally served over couscous, but you may instead serve it over rice or quinoa, with warm flatbread, or on its own.

1 tablespoon olive oil or ¼ cup water

1 large red onion, chopped

1 medium-size carrot, peeled and chopped

1 large green, red, or yellow bell pepper, seeded and chopped

1 large Yukon gold potato, peeled or scrubbed, diced

2 garlic cloves, minced

1 teaspoon grated fresh ginger

1 teaspoon smoked paprika

½ teaspoon ground turmeric

¼ teaspoon cayenne pepper

1 (14.5-ounce) can diced tomatoes, undrained

2 cups vegetable broth

Salt

½ cup dried apricots

¼ cup pitted green olives, halved or sliced

Zest of 1 lemon

3 cups cooked chickpeas or 2 (15.5-ounce) cans chickpeas, rinsed and drained

3 tablespoons minced fresh cilantro or Italian parsley

1. Heat the oil or water in a large saucepan over medium heat. Add the onion and carrot, cover, and cook until softened, about 5 minutes. Add the bell pepper, potato, garlic, ginger, paprika, turmeric, cayenne, tomatoes with their juices, broth, and salt to taste. Reduce the heat to low, and simmer for 25 minutes.

2. Meanwhile, soak the apricots in hot water for 10 minutes, then drain and finely chop. Add the apricots, olives, lemon zest, and chickpeas to the vegetable mixture and cook until hot and the flavors are blended, about 5 minutes. Use the back of a large spoon to crush some of the chickpeas and potatoes and blend into the sauce. Stir in the cilantro, and serve hot.

SERVES 4

nigerian black-eyed peas and greens

THIS RECIPE WAS INSPIRED by a Nigerian dish called *wake-ewa*, which is made with black-eyed peas. This recipe is especially good served over brown basmati rice.

1 tablespoon olive oil or ¼ cup water

1 large yellow onion, chopped

2 tablespoons tomato paste

1 teaspoon dried thyme

1 teaspoon chili powder

1 teaspoon smoked paprika

1 teaspoon ground coriander

½ teaspoon cayenne pepper

½ teaspoon natural sugar

½ teaspoon salt

1 (14.5-ounce) can fire-roasted diced tomatoes, undrained

8 cups chopped stemmed kale or other dark leafy greens

¾ cup vegetable broth or water

3 cups cooked black-eyed peas or 2 (15.5-ounce) cans black-eyed peas, rinsed and drained

3 tablespoons chopped fresh cilantro

Heat the oil or water in a large skillet over medium heat. Add the onion and cook until softened, about 5 minutes. Stir in the tomato paste, thyme, chili powder, paprika, coriander, cayenne, sugar, salt, and tomatoes with their juices and bring to a boil. Reduce the heat to a simmer, add the kale and broth, and cook, stirring frequently, for 10 minutes. Add the black-eyed peas and cook until the vegetables are tender and the flavors are blended, about 10 minutes longer. Sprinkle with the cilantro and serve hot.

SERVES 4

garden vegetable bean stew

Gluten-free | Soy-free option

THIS STEW RELIES on a cornucopia of fresh vegetables for its texture and flavor. It's a great way to make sure everyone eats their vegetables. Vary the vegetables according to your taste—for soy-free, use lima beans instead of edamame.

1 tablespoon olive oil or ¼ cup water

1 large red onion, chopped

1 large carrot, peeled and diced

3 small new potatoes, quartered, or cut into ½-inch dice if larger

1 small red or yellow bell pepper, seeded and diced

1 celery rib, chopped

3 garlic cloves, minced

1 jalapeño chile, seeded and minced

2 small zucchini, diced

1½ cups fresh or frozen corn kernels

1½ cups fresh or frozen shelled edamame or baby lima beans

2 cups vegetable broth

1 (14.5-ounce) can fire-roasted diced tomatoes, undrained

1 teaspoon salt

1 teaspoon dried basil

½ teaspoon dried marjoram

½ teaspoon dried oregano

1 large tomato, chopped

2 tablespoons minced fresh Italian parsley or basil

1. Heat the oil or water in a large pot over medium heat. Add the onion, carrot, potatoes, bell pepper, celery, garlic, and jalapeño. Cover, and cook, stirring occasionally, until the vegetables begin to soften, about 10 minutes, adding a little water if the vegetables begin to stick. Stir in the zucchini, corn, edamame, broth, fire-roasted tomatoes with their juices, salt, basil, marjoram, and oregano. Bring to a boil, lower the heat, and simmer until the vegetables are tender, about 30 minutes.

2. Stir in the fresh tomato, sprinkle with the parsley, and serve hot.

SERVES 4

hot salsa pinto beans and rice

THIS RECIPE IS GREAT over cooked rice or quinoa, so if you have some on hand, dinner can be ready in minutes. Or, instead of serving over a grain, you may spoon the beans into a warm flour or corn tortilla before adding the toppings. For an even quicker version of this dish, simply combine a jar of prepared salsa with the canned pinto beans in a saucepan, stir over medium heat until heated through, and serve. For a soy-free option, use soy-free vegan sour cream.

1 tablespoon olive oil or ¼ cup water

1 large yellow onion, chopped

1 rib celery, chopped

1 large green bell pepper, seeded and chopped

2 large garlic cloves, minced

1 or 2 jalapeño chiles, seeded and minced

2 tablespoons tomato paste

½ teaspoon ground cumin

¼ teaspoon dried oregano

½ teaspoon salt

¼ teaspoon cayenne pepper

1 (28-ounce) can diced tomatoes, drained

1½ cups vegetable broth

3 cups cooked pinto beans or 2 (15.5-ounce) cans pinto beans, rinsed and drained

3 cups hot cooked brown rice

2 cups finely shredded romaine lettuce

½ cup vegan sour cream, purchased or homemade (page 101)

¼ cup sliced pitted black olives

Heat the oil or water in a large saucepan over medium heat. Add the onion, celery, bell pepper, garlic, and jalapeños and cook, stirring occasionally, until softened, about 5 minutes. Stir in the tomato paste, cumin, oregano, salt, and cayenne, then add the tomatoes and broth and bring to a simmer. Add the pinto beans and cook for 10 minutes to heat through and blend the flavors. Serve over the hot rice and top with the lettuce, sour cream, and olives.

SERVES 4

cuban black beans and rice

THE SPANISH NAME for this classic Cuban dish is *moros y cristianos*, or "Moors and Christians." Since the beans are traditionally served on top of the rice, the rice must be cooked separately. White rice is classic, but brown rice is more nutritious.

1 tablespoon olive oil or ¼ cup water

1 medium-size onion, minced

½ medium-size green bell pepper, seeded and minced

1 medium-size zucchini, minced

3 garlic cloves, minced

1 jalapeño chile (optional), seeded and minced

1 tablespoon tomato paste

½ teaspoon ground cumin

½ teaspoon dried oregano

1 (14.5-ounce) can fire-roasted diced tomatoes, undrained

3 cups cooked black beans or 2 (15.5-ounce) cans black beans, rinsed and drained

½ teaspoon salt

Freshly ground black pepper

Hot cooked rice, for serving

Heat the oil or water in a large saucepan over medium heat. Add the onion, bell pepper, zucchini, garlic, and jalapeño (if using). Cover, and cook until the vegetables begin to soften, about 5 minutes. Stir in the tomato paste, cumin, and oregano, and cook for 30 seconds. Add the tomatoes with their juices, beans, salt, and pepper to taste. Cook, uncovered, stirring occasionally, until the vegetables are tender, about 15 minutes. Taste and adjust the seasonings if needed. Serve over the hot cooked rice.

SERVES 4

risotto with artichokes and mushrooms

Gluten-free | Soy-free

ITALIAN PORCINI MUSHROOMS, also called cèpes, add a rich flavor and an authentic touch to this elegant risotto. If unavailable, substitute cremini, portobello, or white button mushrooms.

1 tablespoon olive oil

1 small yellow onion, minced

1½ cups uncooked Arborio rice

4 ounces porcini or other mushrooms, chopped (about 1 cup)

¼ cup dry white wine

4 cups hot vegetable broth

1 cup chopped canned or thawed frozen artichoke hearts

Salt and freshly ground black pepper

1. In a large saucepan, heat the oil over medium heat. Add the onion and sauté, stirring frequently, until soft and golden brown, about 5 minutes. Add the rice and mushrooms and stir until coated with oil and the rice turns translucent, about 5 minutes. Add the wine and simmer gently, stirring occasionally, until it has been absorbed.

2. Add ½ cup of the hot broth and cook, stirring constantly, until all of the liquid has been absorbed. Adjust the heat as necessary to maintain a simmer. Continue cooking, adding hot broth ½ cup at a time and stirring until it is absorbed, until the rice is tender but still firm and the risotto is thick and creamy, about 25 minutes (you may not need all of the broth).

3. About 10 minutes before the rice is finished, stir in the artichoke hearts. When the risotto is finished, remove from the heat and season to taste with salt and pepper. Serve immediately in shallow bowls.

SERVES 4

bombay beans with chutney

Gluten-free | Soy-free

SERVE THIS FRAGRANT, INDIAN-STYLE mélange over basmati rice garnished with vegan yogurt, minced scallions, or chopped peanuts or cashews. Instead of green beans, you could use zucchini or small cauliflower florets. For another variation, try chickpeas instead of the kidney beans.

1 tablespoon olive oil or ¼ cup water

1 large onion, chopped

2 garlic cloves, minced

8 ounces green beans, trimmed and cut into 1-inch pieces (about 2 cups)

1 large red bell pepper, seeded and chopped

1 jalapeño chile, seeded and minced (optional)

1 tablespoon curry powder

½ teaspoon ground cumin

½ teaspoon ground coriander

¼ teaspoon cayenne pepper

2 tablespoons tomato paste

1 (28-ounce) can diced tomatoes, undrained

3 cups cooked dark red kidney beans or 2 (15.5-ounce) cans dark red kidney beans, rinsed and drained

1 cup vegetable broth

Salt

½ cup mango chutney

1. Heat the oil or water in a large pot over medium heat. Add the onion, garlic, green beans, bell pepper, and jalapeño (if using), cover, and cook until softened, about 5 minutes. Stir in the curry powder, cumin, coriander, cayenne, and tomato paste. Add the tomatoes with their juices, kidney beans, broth, and salt to taste. Bring to a boil, then reduce the heat to a simmer and cook until the vegetables are tender, about 30 minutes.

2. Stir in the chutney and simmer until the desired consistency is reached, about 10 minutes longer. Serve hot.

SERVES 6

brown rice and white beans with shiitakes and spinach

THIS HOMEY PILAF IS infinitely versatile. Instead of rice, you can make it with quinoa, wheat berries, or bulgur. You can also swap out the white beans for cooked lentils, black-eyed peas, or chopped seitan. Or add some heat with a minced jalapeño chile.

1 tablespoon olive oil or ¼ cup water

1 large sweet onion, chopped

3 garlic cloves, minced

8 ounces shiitake mushrooms, stemmed and sliced (about 2 cups)

1¼ cups brown rice

2 cups vegetable broth

Salt and freshly ground black pepper

4 scallions, chopped

8 ounces fresh baby spinach (about 8 cups)

1½ cups cooked white beans or 1 (15.5-ounce) can white beans, drained and rinsed

1 tablespoon minced fresh dill or basil

1. Heat the oil or water in a large saucepan over medium heat. Add the onion and cook until soft, about 7 minutes. Add the garlic and mushrooms and cook about 3 minutes or until the mushrooms are tender. Stir in the rice and cook, stirring, for 1 to 2 minutes. Stir in the vegetable broth and bring to a boil. Reduce the heat, season with salt and pepper to taste, cover, and simmer for 35 minutes, stirring occasionally.

2. Uncover, and add the scallions and spinach, stirring until the spinach wilts. Stir in the beans and dill. Cook for 5 minutes longer, or until the broth is absorbed and the rice is tender. Taste and adjust the seasonings if needed. Serve hot.

SERVES 4

greek spinach rice
with white beans

CREAMY CANNELLINI BEANS add protein to this dish inspired by Greek *spanakorizo*, or "spinach rice." It can be made with either long- or short-grain rice, depending on your preference, but I prefer long-grain brown rice. To add color and flavor, garnish with chopped ripe tomatoes, pitted kalamata olives, and/or vegan feta.

1 tablespoon olive oil or ¼ cup water

1 small red onion, finely chopped

1¼ cups uncooked long-grain brown rice

3 cups vegetable broth

1 teaspoon minced fresh oregano
  or ½ teaspoon dried oregano

½ teaspoon salt

⅛ teaspoon freshly ground black pepper

Pinch of ground nutmeg

4 cups chopped fresh spinach

1½ cups cooked cannellini beans
  or 1 (15.5-ounce) can cannellini beans,
  rinsed and drained

3 tablespoons chopped fresh mint

1. Heat the oil or water in a large skillet over medium heat. Add the onion and cook until softened, about 5 minutes. Add the rice, broth, oregano, salt, pepper, and nutmeg and bring to a boil. Reduce the heat to low, cover, and simmer until the rice is almost tender, about 25 minutes.

2. Stir in the spinach and beans and continue cooking until the rice is tender and all of the liquid has been absorbed, 5 to 10 minutes longer.

3. Stir in the mint, remove from the heat, and allow to stand for 5 minutes. Fluff with a fork and serve hot.

SERVES 4

Savory Herb Biscuits

Soy-free

WHEN LYNDSAY ORWIG was helping me test the chili and soup recipes for this book, she'd often comment that she made a batch of her biscuits as an accompaniment, since her boyfriend, Jay, asked for them almost every night. This is Lyndsay's version of a recipe that she originally got from a coworker a few years ago—and she has been making these delicious and easy biscuits ever since. She especially likes them seasoned with oregano, but another herb, such as basil, chives, or thyme (or a combination), would work well too. They're also great without any added herbs.

1⅔ cups all-purpose flour

3 teaspoons baking powder

1 teaspoon salt

½ teaspoon dried oregano or 1 teaspoon fresh oregano (optional)

⅔ cup plain unsweetened nondairy milk

⅓ cup vegetable oil

1. Preheat the oven to 475°F. Lightly oil a large baking sheet and set aside.

2. In a large mixing bowl, combine the flour, baking powder, salt, and oregano (if using). Mix well. Form a well in the center of the mixture, and add the milk and oil. Mix well until the dough comes together—make sure to get all of the flour clinging to the side of the bowl.

3. Use a ¼-cup measuring cup to scoop out the dough (it also helps make a nice biscuit shape) and place the scoops of dough on the prepared baking sheet, arranging the biscuits 1 inch apart. Bake until the biscuits are golden on top and slightly brown on the bottom, about 10 minutes.

MAKES 6 TO 8 BISCUITS

chili today

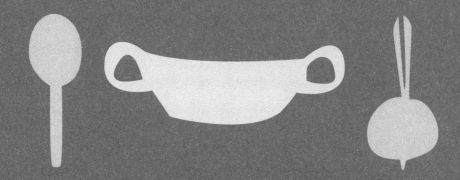

three-bean quinoa chili

Gluten-free | Soy-free

THIS WHOLESOME AND SATISFYING CHILI has it all: whole grains, protein-rich beans, lots of vegetables, and—most important—great flavor. What more could one want from a chili?

1 tablespoon olive oil or ¼ cup water

1 medium-size yellow onion, chopped

1 medium-size zucchini, finely chopped

3 garlic cloves, minced

6 ounces mushrooms, chopped

3 tablespoons hot chili powder

½ teaspoon ground cumin

½ teaspoon dried oregano

Salt and freshly ground black pepper

½ cup uncooked quinoa, rinsed and drained

1 (15.5-ounce) can crushed tomatoes

1 (14.5-ounce) can fire-roasted diced tomatoes, undrained

1 cup vegetable broth or water

1½ cups cooked pinto beans or 1 (15.5-ounce) can pinto beans, rinsed and drained

1½ cups cooked dark red kidney beans or 1 (15.5-ounce) can dark red kidney beans, rinsed and drained

1½ cups cooked black beans or 1 (15.5-ounce) can black beans, rinsed and drained

3 tablespoons chopped fresh cilantro, for serving (optional)

Lime wedges, for serving (optional)

1. Heat the oil or water in a large pot over medium heat. Add the onion and zucchini, cover, and cook until softened, about 5 minutes. Stir in the garlic and mushrooms and cook for 2 minutes longer, then stir in the chili powder, cumin, oregano, and salt and pepper to taste. Add the quinoa, crushed tomatoes, diced tomatoes with their juices, and broth, and bring to a boil. Reduce the heat to a simmer, cover, and cook for 15 minutes.

2. Add the pinto, kidney, and black beans, and simmer, uncovered, for 30 minutes longer, stirring occasionally.

3. Taste and adjust the seasonings if needed. Serve hot, accompanied by cilantro and lime wedges, if using.

SERVES 4

garlic lover's chili

THE ABUNDANCE OF GARLIC combined with the other spices adds to the rich complexity of flavor in this delicious chili. I like to serve it over pasta or with hot, crusty garlic bread and a salad.

1 tablespoon olive oil or ¼ cup water

1 medium-size yellow onion, chopped

1 red bell pepper, seeded and chopped

8 garlic cloves, minced

8 ounces tempeh, steamed and chopped (see page 6)

¼ cup tomato paste

1 (28-ounce) can diced tomatoes, undrained

1½ cups low-sodium tomato juice or water

3 cups cooked dark red kidney beans or 2 (15.5-ounce) cans dark red kidney beans, rinsed and drained

1 (4-ounce) can diced mild green chiles, drained

1 tablespoon wheat-free tamari

2 tablespoons hot chili powder

1 teaspoon dried oregano

½ teaspoon dried marjoram

½ teaspoon dried basil

½ teaspoon red pepper flakes

¾ teaspoon salt

¼ teaspoon freshly ground black pepper

½ cup sliced pitted black olives

1. Heat the oil or water in a large pot over medium heat. Add the onion, bell pepper, and garlic. Cover and cook until softened, about 5 minutes. Remove the lid and stir in the tempeh, tomato paste, tomatoes with their juices, tomato juice, beans, chiles, tamari, chili powder, oregano, marjoram, basil, red pepper flakes, salt, and pepper. Bring to a boil, then reduce the heat to a simmer and cook for about 45 minutes.

2. Just before serving, add the olives, then taste and adjust the seasonings if needed. Serve hot.

SERVES 4

cincinnati chili

CINCINNATI CHILI IS KNOWN FOR being served in several "ways," as in 3-way on up to 5-way chili. To streamline this chili, the cooked kidney beans are added to the chili rather than prepared separately, as is traditional. Oyster crackers and hot sauce are classic accompaniments. Note: To reconstitute TVP, combine 1 cup TVP granules with 1 cup hot water and set aside for 10 minutes before adding to the recipe. If you prefer to go gluten-free or soy-free, you may substitute 1½ cups cooked beans or lentils for the seitan or TVP. If you're gluten-sensitive, be sure to also check the labels on the vegan Worcestershire sauce and other ingredients to be sure they're gluten-free.

1 tablespoon olive oil or ¼ cup water

1 large yellow onion, finely chopped

3 garlic cloves, minced

2 tablespoons tomato paste

8 ounces seitan, finely chopped

1 cup TVP granules, reconstituted (see headnote)

2 tablespoons chili powder

1 tablespoon unsweetened cocoa powder

2 teaspoons paprika

1 teaspoon ground cinnamon

1 teaspoon salt

½ teaspoon ground cumin

½ teaspoon cayenne pepper

½ teaspoon ground allspice

½ teaspoon dried marjoram

½ teaspoon freshly ground black pepper

½ teaspoon ground coriander

3 cups cooked dark red kidney beans or 2 (15.5-ounce) cans dark red kidney beans, rinsed and drained

1 cup vegetable broth or water, plus more if needed

1 cup tomato sauce

2 tablespoons ketchup

1 tablespoon cider vinegar

1 teaspoon vegan Worcestershire sauce

1 teaspoon agave nectar

8 ounces spaghetti, cooked and kept warm

1 medium-size yellow onion, minced, for serving

Shredded vegan cheddar cheese or Cheddah Sauce (recipe follows), for serving

1. Heat the oil or water in a large pot over medium heat. Add the onion, cover, and cook until softened, about 5 minutes. Stir in the garlic and cook for 30 seconds, then add the tomato paste, seitan, and reconstituted TVP and cook for 2 minutes longer. Add the chili powder, cocoa, paprika, cinnamon, salt, cumin, cayenne, allspice, marjoram, black pepper, and coriander. Stir in the beans and broth, then add the tomato sauce, ketchup, vinegar, vegan Worcestershire, and agave. Bring just to a boil, then reduce the heat to low and cook, uncovered, for 35 to 45 minutes, stirring occasionally. Add additional broth if the chili becomes too thick. Taste and adjust the seasonings if needed.

2. To serve, spread a layer of cooked spaghetti on individual serving plates (oval plates are traditional). Ladle the chili over the spaghetti and top with the minced onion, then sprinkle with vegan cheddar and serve hot.

SERVES 4

CHEDDAH SAUCE

Soy-free option

If you're not a fan of commercial vegan cheese products, you can make your own cheesy sauce using this recipe. For a soy-free version, omit the miso paste.

1 russet potato, peeled and cut into 1-inch dice

1 carrot, peeled and cut into ¼-inch slices

1 cup vegetable broth, plus more if needed

½ cup nutritional yeast

2 tablespoons tahini

1 teaspoon mellow white miso paste

½ teaspoon Dijon mustard

½ teaspoon ground turmeric

½ teaspoon onion powder

1 cup plain unsweetened nondairy milk, plus more if needed

1 tablespoon rice vinegar

Salt to taste

Combine the potato, carrot, and broth in a small saucepan. Cover and cook over medium heat until the vegetables are tender, about 10 minutes. Transfer the mixture to a high-speed blender or food processor. Add all of the remaining ingredients and process until well blended. For a thinner sauce, add more liquid (broth or nondairy milk). For a thicker sauce, transfer to a saucepan and bring just to a boil, then stir in a slurry (1 tablespoon cornstarch or arrowroot mixed with 1 tablespoon water) and cook until thickened. Taste and adjust the seasonings if needed.

MAKES ABOUT 3 ½ CUPS

black bean and sweet potato chili

Gluten-free | Soy-free

GREAT ANYTIME, THIS CHILI is especially fun to make for Halloween owing to the festive colors of the black beans and bright orange sweet potatoes. Butternut squash may be used instead of the sweet potatoes, if desired.

1 tablespoon olive oil or ¼ cup water

1 large onion, chopped

3 garlic cloves, minced

1½ pounds sweet potatoes, peeled and cut into ½-inch dice

2 chipotle chiles in adobo, minced

1 (14.5-ounce) can fire-roasted diced tomatoes, undrained

1 (14.5-ounce) can crushed tomatoes

1½ cups vegetable broth, plus more if needed

3 tablespoons chili powder

1 teaspoon ground cumin

1 teaspoon ground coriander

½ teaspoon dried oregano

1 teaspoon salt

3 cups cooked black beans or 2 (15.5-ounce) cans black beans, rinsed and drained

1. Heat the oil or water in a large pot over medium heat. Add the onion and garlic, cover, and cook, stirring occasionally, until softened, about 10 minutes. Add the sweet potatoes, chipotles, diced tomatoes with their juices, crushed tomatoes, broth, chili powder, cumin, coriander, oregano, salt, and beans. Stir to combine, then bring to a boil. Reduce the heat to low, cover, and simmer, stirring occasionally, until the vegetables are tender, about 45 minutes.

2. Add more broth if the chili is too thick for your taste. If you prefer a thicker chili, cook uncovered for 15 minutes to thicken. Serve hot.

SERVES 4 TO 6

sweet and spicy chili

RAISINS, CINNAMON, AND SLIVERED ALMONDS give this chili an exotic nuance. You might try an aromatic rice such as jasmine or basmati to complement the hint of sweetness in the chili.

1 tablespoon olive oil or ¼ cup water

1 medium-size yellow onion, chopped

1 carrot, peeled and finely chopped

1 red bell pepper, seeded and chopped

2 garlic cloves, minced

2 jalapeño chiles, seeded and minced,
    or 2 chipotle chiles in adobo, minced

3 tablespoons chili powder

1 teaspoon natural sugar

1 teaspoon salt

1 teaspoon ground cumin

1 teaspoon ground coriander

½ teaspoon ground cinnamon

⅛ teaspoon cayenne pepper

¼ cup tomato paste

1 (14.5-ounce) can diced tomatoes, undrained

1½ cups apple juice

3 cups cooked dark red kidney beans
    or 2 (15.5-ounce) cans dark red kidney
    beans, rinsed and drained

¼ cup raisins

¼ cup slivered toasted almonds

1. Heat the oil or water in a large pot over medium heat. Add the onion, carrot, bell pepper, and garlic. Cover and cook until softened, about 5 minutes. Stir in the chiles, chili powder, sugar, salt, cumin, coriander, cinnamon, and cayenne. Add the tomato paste and tomatoes with their juices. Stir in the apple juice, then add the beans and raisins and bring to a boil. Reduce the heat to a simmer and cook, uncovered, for 30 minutes.

2. Taste and adjust the seasonings if needed. Sprinkle with the almonds and serve hot.

SERVES 4

tequila sundown chili

Gluten-free | Soy-free

TEQUILA AND LIME DELIVER a pungent kick and orange juice adds a subtle sweetness to this party chili. Serve it with your favorite toppings and side dishes, along with a pitcher of tequila sunrises, or maybe some cold beer served in glasses rimmed with lime juice and sea salt.

1 tablespoon olive oil or ¼ cup water

1 large yellow onion, chopped

2 garlic cloves, minced

2 tablespoons chili powder

1 teaspoon ground coriander

1 teaspoon dried savory

½ teaspoon dried marjoram

¼ cup tequila

1 (14.5-ounce) can crushed tomatoes

1 (14.5-ounce) can diced fire-roasted tomatoes, undrained

1 cup vegetable broth or water

3 cups cooked pinto beans or 2 (15.5-ounce) cans pinto beans, rinsed and drained

1 teaspoon natural sugar

1 teaspoon salt

¼ teaspoon freshly ground black pepper

¼ cup freshly squeezed orange juice

2 tablespoons freshly squeezed lime juice

1. Heat the oil or water in a large pot over medium heat. Add the onion, garlic, chili powder, coriander, savory, and marjoram. Cook, stirring, until softened, 3 to 5 minutes. Stir in the tequila, then add the crushed tomatoes, diced tomatoes with their juices, broth, beans, sugar, salt, and pepper. Bring to a boil, then reduce the heat to a simmer and cook until the vegetables are tender, 30 to 40 minutes.

2. Stir in the orange juice and lime juice and simmer until the desired consistency is reached, 5 to 10 minutes longer. Taste and adjust the seasonings if needed. Serve hot.

SERVES 4

orange-scented chipotle chili

THIS RICH, AROMATIC CHILI is fragrant with orange and smoky hot from the chipotle and paprika. Try it served over basmati rice, accompanied by a crisp white wine. This chili can be gluten- and soy-free if you omit the optional vegan sausage.

1 tablespoon olive oil or ¼ cup water

1 large onion, chopped

1 red or orange bell pepper, seeded and chopped

3 garlic cloves, minced

3 tablespoons chili powder

1 teaspoon smoked paprika

½ teaspoon minced fresh marjoram or ½ teaspoon dried marjoram

2 tablespoons tomato paste

2 teaspoons pure maple syrup

2 chipotle chiles in adobo, minced

1 (14.5-ounce) can fire-roasted diced tomatoes, undrained

3 cups cooked black beans or 2 (15.5-ounce) cans black beans, rinsed and drained

1 cup vegetable broth

½ cup freshly squeezed orange juice

2 teaspoons fresh orange zest

1 teaspoon liquid smoke

2 vegan sausage links, chopped and lightly browned (optional)

Salt and freshly ground black pepper

1 ripe Hass avocado, for serving

3 tablespoons chopped fresh cilantro, for serving

1. Heat the oil or water in a large pot over medium heat. Add the onion, bell pepper, and garlic. Cover and cook until softened, about 5 minutes. Stir in the chili powder, paprika, marjoram, tomato paste, and maple syrup. Add the chipotles, tomatoes with their juices, beans, and broth and bring to a boil. Reduce the heat to a simmer and cook, uncovered, for 20 minutes.

2. Stir in the orange juice, orange zest, liquid smoke, and sausage (if using). Season to taste with salt and pepper and simmer for 10 minutes longer, adding a little water if the chili becomes too dry. When ready to serve, pit, peel, and dice the avocado. Top the chili with the avocado and cilantro and serve hot.

SERVES 4

blazing bulgur chili

THE SWEETNESS OF THE CORN helps to offset some of the chile's heat, but you'll still want to plan a few "cool-down" accompaniments for this fiery chili, such as vegan sour cream and chopped avocados. True fire-eaters may want to increase the number of chiles or add a habanero or Scotch bonnet to the pot.

1 cup water

¾ cup medium-grind bulgur

1 tablespoon olive oil or ¼ cup water

1 small red onion, minced

1 or 2 serrano or jalapeño chiles, seeded and minced

1 large portobello mushroom cap, cut into ½-inch dice

3 tablespoons hot chili powder

1 teaspoon ground cumin

1 teaspoon smoked paprika

½ teaspoon dried basil

3 cups cooked pinto beans or 2 (15.5-ounce) cans pinto beans, rinsed and drained

1 (14.5-ounce) can crushed tomatoes

1 (14.5-ounce) can fire-roasted diced tomatoes, undrained

1 cup vegetable broth, water, or low-sodium tomato juice, plus more if needed

1 cup fresh or frozen corn kernels

1. Bring 1 cup of water to a boil in a saucepan. Add the bulgur and salt to taste. Remove from the heat, cover, and set aside.

2. Heat the oil or ¼ cup water in a large pot over medium heat. Add the onion, chile, and diced mushroom, and cook until softened, about 5 minutes. Add the chili powder, cumin, paprika, basil, beans, crushed tomatoes, diced tomatoes with their juices, and broth. Bring to a boil, then reduce the heat to a simmer, stir in the corn and bulgur, and cook for 30 to 45 minutes. Add more liquid if the chili becomes too thick.

3. Taste and adjust the seasonings if needed. Serve hot.

SERVES 4

How Do You Serve Chili?

JUST AS THERE ARE COUNTLESS ways to make chili, there are also many different ways to serve it. The simplest way is to serve it alone in a bowl, as you would a hearty soup or stew, accompanied by crackers. Sometimes chili is accompanied by cornbread. Some traditions call for spooning chili over pasta or rice. Chili is also good served with tortilla chips or the biscuits on page 87.

Then there are the toppings. Everything from diced avocado, sliced olives, and minced onion to vegan sour cream and shredded cheese might find its way to the top of your favorite chili. A crisp green salad makes a great accompaniment as well. For the recipes in this chapter, I've included a variety of serving suggestions, but if your preferences lean another way, I encourage you to serve chili "your way."

chili java

THE ADDITION OF STRONG BLACK COFFEE adds a hearty richness to this chili. It is said that chuck wagon cooks of the Old West often used leftover coffee in their cooking to conserve their supply of fresh water. Note: To reconstitute TVP, combine 1 cup TVP granules with 1 cup hot water and set aside for 10 minutes before adding to the recipe. Instead of using TVP, you may substitute chopped seitan, tempeh, or vegan sausage.

1 tablespoon olive oil or ¼ cup water

1 medium-size onion, chopped

2 garlic cloves, minced

3 tablespoons chili powder

1 teaspoon ground cumin

¾ cup strong brewed coffee

¾ cup vegetable broth or water

1 cup TVP granules, reconstituted (see headnote)

3 cups cooked dark red kidney beans or 2 (15.5-ounce) cans dark red kidney beans, rinsed and drained

1 (4-ounce) can diced mild green chiles, drained

1 tablespoon chopped fresh cilantro

Salt and freshly ground black pepper

1 ripe Hass avocado, for serving (optional)

Vegan sour cream, purchased or homemade (recipe follows), for serving

1. Heat the oil or water in a large pot over medium heat. Add the onion and garlic, cover, and cook until softened, about 5 minutes. Stir in the chili powder, cumin, coffee, and broth. Bring to a boil, then reduce the heat to a simmer. Add the reconstituted TVP, beans, and chiles, and cook for 45 minutes, stirring occasionally.

2. Stir in the cilantro and salt and pepper to taste, and simmer for 5 minutes longer. If using the avocado, when ready to serve, pit, peel, and dice it. Top each serving with a dollop of the sour cream and some of the avocado, and serve hot.

SERVES 4

VEGAN SOUR CREAM

Gluten-free | Soy-free option

There are some very good commercial vegan sour cream products available, but if you prefer to make your own, try this recipe. You can make this soy-free by using white beans or cashews instead of the silken tofu.

½ cup cooked silken tofu, white beans, or soaked and drained raw cashews

1½ tablespoons freshly squeezed lemon juice

1 tablespoon rice vinegar

2 teaspoons tahini

½ teaspoon salt

Combine all of the ingredients in a high-speed blender or food processor and process until completely smooth. Taste and adjust the seasonings if needed.

MAKES ABOUT ¾ CUP

chili verde

Gluten-free | Soy-free

FRESH TOMATILLOS LOOK LIKE small green tomatoes in papery husks, and they have a slightly tart flavor. If fresh ones are unavailable, use the canned variety. Salsa verde, a green salsa, is available in most supermarkets. I use less chili powder than usual in this recipe to try to retain as much of the green color of the chili as possible. If you prefer additional chili powder, add it according to taste. When Lori Maffei tested the recipe, we discussed how nice it would be to have white chili powder and—guess what?—she found some online! I haven't tried it yet, but it sounds intriguing.

1 tablespoon olive oil or ¼ cup water

1 medium-size yellow onion, chopped

3 garlic cloves, minced

1 large green bell pepper, seeded and chopped

1 medium-size zucchini, chopped

1 or 2 jalapeño chiles, seeded and minced

1½ cups husked and chopped tomatillos, or 1 (14-ounce) can tomatillos, drained and chopped

1 cup salsa verde

1 to 2 tablespoons chili powder

1 teaspoon dried oregano

1 teaspoon ground cumin

Salt and freshly ground black pepper

1½ cups vegetable broth or water, plus more if needed

3 cups cooked Great Northern or other white beans or 2 (15.5-ounce) cans Great Northern or other white beans, rinsed and drained

1 ripe Hass avocado, for serving

¼ cup chopped fresh cilantro or Italian parsley, for serving

1. Heat the oil or water in a large pot over medium heat. Add the onion, garlic, bell pepper, zucchini, and jalapeño. Cook, stirring, until the vegetables begin to soften, about 5 minutes. Add the tomatillos, salsa verde, chili powder, oregano, cumin, and salt and pepper to taste.

2. Add the broth and beans, and bring to a boil. Reduce the heat to a simmer, and cook, stirring occasionally, until the vegetables are tender, about 40 minutes. Add more broth if the chili becomes too thick.

3. Taste and adjust the seasonings if needed. When ready to serve, pit, peel, and dice the avocado. Top each serving with avocado and cilantro, and serve hot.

SERVES 4

tex-mex tempeh chili

TEMPEH'S MEAT-LIKE TEXTURE and high protein content make it a natural ingredient for chili. If you're not a fan of tempeh, substitute chopped seitan or reconstituted TVP.

1 tablespoon olive oil or ¼ cup water

1 large yellow onion, chopped

3 garlic cloves, minced

2 jalapeño chiles, seeded and minced

1 pound tempeh, steamed and chopped (see page 6)

3 tablespoons chili powder

1 teaspoon ground cumin

1 teaspoon dried oregano

1 (14.5-ounce) can crushed tomatoes

1 (14.5-ounce) can fire-roasted diced tomatoes, undrained

1½ cups cooked pinto beans or 1 (15.5-ounce) can pinto beans, rinsed and drained

1 cup water

Salt and freshly ground black pepper

1 cup fresh or frozen corn kernels

1. Heat the oil or water in a large pot over medium heat. Add the onion and cook for 5 minutes to soften. Stir in the garlic and jalapeños and cook for about 30 seconds, then stir in the chopped tempeh, chili powder, cumin, and oregano, and cook for 3 to 5 minutes longer. Add the crushed tomatoes, diced tomatoes with their juices, beans, water, and salt and pepper to taste. Bring to a boil, then reduce the heat to a simmer and cook for 30 minutes, stirring occasionally.

2. Add the corn, then taste and adjust the seasonings if needed. Cook until the desired consistency is reached, about 10 minutes longer. Serve hot.

SERVES 4

louisiana bayou chili

FILÉ POWDER, WHICH IS MADE from ground sassafras leaves, is an ingredient found in gumbos and other Creole dishes. It is available in most supermarkets and specialty food shops. If you can't fine filé powder, you can omit it and the chili will still taste great, although the filé does add authentic flavor. Serve this chili over rice, with a bottle of hot sauce on the table for those who like a little extra kick. Note: To reconstitute TVP, combine 1 cup TVP granules with 1 cup hot water and set aside for 10 minutes before adding to the recipe. You can make this soy-free by using lentils instead of TVP.

1 tablespoon olive oil or ¼ cup water

1 red onion, chopped

1 celery rib, minced

1 green bell pepper, seeded and chopped

1 or 2 jalapeño chiles, seeded and minced

3 garlic cloves, minced

3 tablespoons chili powder

1 teaspoon dried thyme

1 teaspoon filé powder

1 (28-ounce) can diced tomatoes, undrained

1 cup TVP granules, reconstituted (see headnote), or cooked lentils

1 cup vegetable broth or water

3 cups cooked red beans or 2 (15.5-ounce) cans red beans, rinsed and drained

1 teaspoon Louisiana hot sauce

⅛ teaspoon cayenne pepper

Salt and freshly ground black pepper

1. Heat the oil or water in a large pot over medium heat. Add the onion, celery, bell pepper, jalapeño, and garlic, and cook until softened, 3 to 5 minutes. Stir in the chili powder, thyme, and filé powder. Add the tomatoes with their juices, reconstituted TVP, and broth. Bring to a boil, then reduce the heat to a simmer. Add the beans, hot sauce, cayenne, and salt and pepper to taste, and cook for 30 minutes longer to blend the flavors, stirring occasionally.

2. Taste and adjust the seasonings if needed. Serve hot.

SERVES 4

west coast chili

FILLED WITH VIBRANT FRESH VEGETABLES and topped with creamy avocado and piquant black olives, this chili is imbued with a West Coast vibe. To complement the mood, serve it with a loaf of San Francisco sourdough bread.

1 tablespoon olive oil or ¼ cup water

1 medium-size red onion, chopped

1 red bell pepper, seeded and chopped

1 yellow bell pepper, seeded and chopped

2 garlic cloves, minced

1 serrano chile, seeded and minced

1 medium-size zucchini, chopped

8 plum tomatoes, diced

¼ cup tomato paste

1 chipotle chile in adobo, minced

3 tablespoons chili powder

½ teaspoon dried oregano

½ teaspoon smoked paprika

Salt

3 cups cooked black beans or 2 (15.5-ounce) cans black beans, rinsed and drained

1 cup vegetable broth, plus more if needed

¼ cup dry red wine (optional)

1 ½ cups fresh or thawed frozen corn kernels

2 ripe Hass avocados, for serving

½ cup sliced pitted ripe olives, for serving

¼ cup chopped fresh cilantro, for serving

1. Heat the oil or water in a large pot over medium heat. Add the onion, red and yellow bell peppers, garlic, and serrano chile. Cover and cook until the vegetables are softened, about 10 minutes. Add the zucchini, tomatoes, tomato paste, chipotle, chili powder, oregano, paprika, and salt to taste. Stir in the beans, broth, and wine (if using). Bring to a boil, then reduce the heat to a simmer and cook until the flavors are blended and the desired consistency is reached, about 30 minutes. Add more broth if the chili becomes too thick.

2. Just before serving, stir in the corn, and pit, peel, and dice the avocados. Top each serving with avocados, olives, and cilantro, and serve hot.

SERVES 4

world's fair chili

THIS MIDWESTERN-STYLE CHILI, with its subtle sweetness and absence of garlic, is inspired by the 1904 St. Louis World's Fair, where chili was introduced to the rest of the world. If you like, instead of tempeh, you may use reconstituted TVP or, to make it soy-free, chopped seitan.

1 tablespoon olive oil or ¼ cup water

1 pound tempeh, steamed (see page 6)

1 large yellow onion, finely chopped

1 (28-ounce) can crushed tomatoes

1 (4-ounce) can diced mild green chiles, drained

1 tablespoon cider vinegar

3 tablespoons chili powder

1 teaspoon natural sugar

1 teaspoon dried oregano

1 teaspoon salt

1 cup low-sodium tomato juice or water

3 cups cooked dark red kidney beans or 2 (15.5-ounce) cans dark red kidney beans, rinsed and drained

1. Heat the oil or water in a large pot over medium heat. Crumble the tempeh and add it to the pot. Cook for 5 minutes, then add the onion and cook until softened, about 5 minutes. Stir in the tomatoes, chiles, vinegar, chili powder, sugar, oregano, and salt. Add the tomato juice and bring to a boil. Reduce the heat to a simmer, add the beans, and cook for 30 minutes.

2. Taste and adjust the seasonings if needed. Serve hot.

SERVES 4

flaming firehouse chili

Gluten-free | Soy-free option

THERE ARE NEARLY AS MANY RECIPES for firehouse chili as there are firehouses. The versatility and ease of preparation of this spicy one-pot meal makes chili a perennial favorite among firehouse cooks. This one gets its heat from hot chili powder and hot salsa to save you the trouble of mincing fresh hot chiles. If your chili powder isn't especially hot, you can spice things up by adding ½ teaspoon (or more) cayenne pepper or your choice of minced fresh or dried hot chiles. Or, for a mild version, use mild chili powder and mild salsa. Serve with cornbread, and offer a choice of cooling toppings, such as shredded vegan cheese, vegan sour cream, and diced avocado. Note: To reconstitute TVP, combine 1 cup TVP granules with 1 cup hot water and set aside for 10 minutes before adding to the recipe. You can make this soy-free by using lentils instead of TVP.

1 tablespoon olive oil or ¼ cup water

1 large yellow onion, chopped

3 garlic cloves, minced

3 tablespoons hot chili powder

1 teaspoon ground cumin

1 cup TVP granules, reconstituted (see headnote), or cooked lentils

1 (14-ounce) can fire-roasted diced tomatoes, undrained

1½ cups hot tomato salsa

1 teaspoon salt

¼ teaspoon freshly ground black pepper

1 cup water, vegetable broth, or beer, plus more if needed

3 cups cooked dark red kidney beans or 2 (15.5-ounce) cans dark red kidney beans, rinsed and drained

1. Heat the oil or water in a large pot over medium heat. Add the onion and garlic, cover, and cook until softened, about 5 minutes. Add the chili powder, cumin, reconstituted TVP, tomatoes with their juices, salsa, salt, pepper, and water. Bring to a boil, then reduce the heat to medium-low. Add the beans and simmer for about 45 minutes, stirring occasionally. Add more water, if necessary, until the desired consistency is reached.

2. Taste and adjust the seasonings if needed. Serve hot.

SERVES 4

beer chaser chili

Gluten-free | Soy-free option

BEER IS AN INGREDIENT in this hot and hearty chili, but it also makes a great chaser to have on hand to douse the fire of this incendiary dish. When Lyndsay Orwig tested this recipe, she used the 1554 Enlightened Black Ale from the New Belgium Brewing Company, after checking on Barnivore.com to discover that it's vegan-friendly. You can use any type of beer that you have on hand, but a dark beer will add more richness of flavor. Note: To reconstitute TVP, combine 1 cup TVP granules with 1 cup hot water and set aside for 10 minutes before adding to the recipe. If you're gluten-sensitive, as always check your labels to be sure ingredients such as vegan Worcestershire sauce and tamari are gluten-free. You can make this soy-free by using lentils instead of TVP and coconut aminos instead of Worcestershire sauce or tamari.

1 tablespoon olive oil or ¼ cup water

1 large red onion, chopped

3 garlic cloves, minced

1 bell pepper (any color), seeded and chopped

2 jalapeño chiles, seeded and minced

3 tablespoons chili powder

½ teaspoon ground cumin

½ teaspoon dried oregano

½ teaspoon smoked paprika

1 tablespoon vegan Worcestershire sauce or wheat-free tamari

1 teaspoon hot pepper sauce

1 cup beer, plus more if needed

1 (28-ounce) can crushed tomatoes

3 cups cooked pinto beans or 2 (15.5-ounce) cans pinto beans, rinsed and drained

1 cup TVP granules, reconstituted (see headnote), or cooked lentils

Salt and freshly ground black pepper

Heat the oil or water in a large pot over medium heat. Add the onion, garlic, bell pepper, and jalapeños and cook until softened, about 5 minutes. Add the chili powder, cumin, oregano, and paprika, and stir to coat. Add the vegan Worcestershire sauce, hot pepper sauce, beer, tomatoes, beans, reconstituted TVP, and salt and pepper to taste. Bring to a boil, then reduce the heat to low and simmer, stirring frequently, until the vegetables are tender and the chili has thickened, about 45 minutes. Add more liquid if the chili becomes too thick. Serve hot.

SERVES 4

devil's food chili

Gluten-free | Soy-free

THE SERRANO CHILES make this chili devilishly hot and spicy. For less heat, remove the seeds and membranes before chopping. If your chili powder isn't hot, add ½ teaspoon or more of cayenne pepper. A soothing guacamole makes a good accompaniment.

1 tablespoon olive oil or ¼ cup water

1 large red onion, chopped

3 garlic cloves, minced

2 serrano chiles, seeded and minced

1 small eggplant, peeled and chopped

8 ounces white mushrooms, chopped

¼ cup tomato paste

1 (28-ounce) can diced tomatoes, undrained

3 tablespoons hot chili powder

1 teaspoon salt

¼ teaspoon freshly ground black pepper

3 cups cooked black beans or 2 (15.5-ounce) cans black beans, rinsed and drained

1 cup vegetable broth or water, plus more if needed

½ cup dry red wine (optional)

¼ cup sliced pitted kalamata olives

1. Heat the oil or water in a large pot over medium heat. Add the onion, garlic, chiles, and eggplant and cook, stirring, until softened, about 7 minutes. Add the mushrooms, tomato paste, tomatoes with their juices, chili powder, salt, and pepper. Stir in the beans, broth, and wine (if using), and bring to a boil. Reduce the heat to a simmer, cover, and cook for 15 minutes, stirring occasionally. Remove the lid and simmer for 30 minutes longer, stirring occasionally. If the chili becomes too thick, stir in additional liquid.

2. Taste and adjust the seasonings if needed. Top with the olives and serve hot.

SERVES 4

texas too-hot chili

TEXAS CHILI OFTEN CONTAINS no beans but two kinds of meat, one cubed and the other ground. Here, cubed seitan and TVP share the pot for the desired textural variations. Note: To reconstitute TVP, combine 1 cup TVP granules with 1 cup hot water and set aside for 10 minutes before adding to the recipe. You can make this soy-free by using lentils instead of TVP and coconut aminos instead of tamari.

1 cup vegan sour cream, purchased or homemade (page 101)

⅓ cup minced fresh cilantro

Salt

1 tablespoon olive oil or ¼ cup water

1 large red onion, minced

3 garlic cloves, minced

8 ounces seitan, cut into ½-inch dice

¼ cup tomato paste

2 chipotle chiles in adobo, minced

1 tablespoon wheat-free tamari

3 tablespoons hot chili powder

1 teaspoon dried oregano

½ teaspoon ground cumin

½ teaspoon hot red pepper flakes

¼ teaspoon freshly ground black pepper

1 cup TVP granules, reconstituted (see headnote), or cooked lentils

1 cup vegetable broth, low-sodium tomato juice, or water

½ cup beer (or additional broth, tomato juice, or water)

1 ripe Hass avocado, for serving (optional)

1. In a small bowl, combine the sour cream, cilantro, and salt to taste. Mix well. Cover and refrigerate until serving time.

2. Heat the oil or water in a large pot over medium heat. Add the onion and garlic cook until softened, about 5 minutes. Add the seitan, tomato paste, chipotles, tamari, chili powder, oregano, cumin, red pepper flakes, black pepper, and salt to taste. Stir in the reconstituted TVP, broth, and beer, and bring to a boil. Reduce the heat to a simmer, cover, and cook until the desired consistency is reached, about 30 minutes.

3. Taste and adjust the seasonings if needed. If using the avocado, pit, peel, and dice it. Ladle the chili into bowls, and top with a spoonful of the cilantro sour cream and some of the avocado. Serve hot.

SERVES 4

spicy vegan sausage and bean chili

SAUSAGE AND MUSHROOMS PROVIDE great texture and flavor elements to this hearty chili. If ancho chiles are unavailable, substitute 2 to 3 tablespoons of your favorite chili powder.

3 dried ancho chiles, stemmed and seeded

1 tablespoon olive oil or ¼ cup water

1 medium-size onion, chopped

3 garlic cloves, minced

2 tablespoons tomato paste

1 (15-ounce) can diced tomatoes, undrained

8 ounces vegan sausage links, chopped

8 ounces white mushrooms, chopped

1 teaspoon dried oregano

½ teaspoon ground cumin

½ teaspoon red pepper flakes

¼ teaspoon cayenne pepper

Salt and freshly ground black pepper

1 cup vegetable broth or water

3 cups cooked pinto beans or 2 (15.5-ounce) cans pinto beans, rinsed and drained

Vegan sour cream, purchased or homemade (page 101), for serving (optional)

1. Grind the anchos to a powder in a spice grinder or food processor.

2. Heat the oil or water in a large pot over medium heat. Add the onion and garlic and cook until softened, about 5 minutes. Stir in the tomato paste, tomatoes with their juices, sausage, mushrooms, ancho powder, oregano, cumin, red pepper flakes, cayenne, and salt and pepper to taste. Cook for 1 to 2 minutes. Add the broth and beans and bring to a boil. Reduce the heat to a simmer and cook until the flavors have blended and the desired consistency is reached, about 40 minutes.

3. Taste and adjust the seasonings if needed. Serve hot, topped with vegan sour cream, if using.

SERVES 4

sautés and stir-fries

jamaican-style coconut rice bowl

Gluten-free | Soy-free

ALTHOUGH THERE ARE many variations of this traditional dish throughout the Caribbean, it's a special favorite in Jamaica, where the "peas" used are actually red kidney beans. Coconut milk and chile peppers add richness and heat to this tasty and nutritious version, which can be ready in minutes if you use cooked rice and canned beans. Accompany with a salad or green vegetable.

2 teaspoons olive oil or ¼ cup water

1 medium-size red or yellow onion, chopped

1 russet or sweet potato, peeled and cut into ½-inch dice

½ red or green bell pepper, seeded and chopped

3 garlic cloves, chopped

1 or 2 small hot chiles, seeded and chopped

1 teaspoon minced fresh thyme or ½ teaspoon dried thyme

2 cups small broccoli florets

1 medium-size zucchini, cut into ½-inch dice

1 (13-ounce) can unsweetened coconut milk

1½ cups cooked dark red kidney beans or 1 (15.5-ounce) can dark red kidney beans, rinsed and drained

Salt and freshly ground black pepper

3 cups hot cooked rice, for serving

Lime wedges, for serving (optional)

1. Heat the oil or water in a large pot over medium heat. Add the onion, potato, bell pepper, garlic, and chile, and sauté for 5 minutes to soften. Add the thyme, broccoli, zucchini, and coconut milk, stirring to combine, then stir in the beans and season to taste with salt and pepper. Cover and cook over medium-low heat, stirring occasionally, until the vegetables are tender, 12 to 15 minutes.

2. Taste and adjust the seasonings if needed. Serve over the rice in shallow bowls with a squeeze of lime, if desired.

SERVES 4

tunisian chickpeas with sweet potatoes and greens

THIS SATISFYING RECIPE is a complete meal as is, but it is also good served over couscous, rice, or quinoa or accompanied by warm flatbread.

1 tablespoon olive oil or ¼ cup water

1 medium-size yellow onion, chopped

4 cloves garlic, minced

1 large or 2 medium-size sweet potatoes, peeled and cut into ½-inch dice

1½ teaspoons ground coriander

1 teaspoon smoked paprika

½ teaspoon dried thyme

½ teaspoon ground cumin

½ teaspoon red pepper flakes

Salt and freshly ground black pepper

1 (14.5-ounce) can fire-roasted diced tomatoes, undrained

1½ cups cooked chickpeas or 1 (15.5-ounce) can chickpeas, rinsed and drained

½ cup vegetable broth or water

6 to 8 cups chopped stemmed kale, spinach, or chard

Lemon wedges, for serving

1. Heat the oil or water in a large pot over medium heat. Add the onion and garlic and cook for 3 to 5 minutes to soften, stirring occasionally. Add the sweet potato, coriander, paprika, thyme, cumin, red pepper flakes, and salt and pepper to taste. Add the tomatoes with their juices, chickpeas, and broth, and bring to a boil. Reduce the heat to a simmer and cook for 10 minutes.

2. Add the kale, stirring to wilt. Simmer until the vegetables are tender, another 10 to 15 minutes. Serve hot with a squeeze of lemon.

SERVES 4

szechwan tempeh and green beans

SPICY HOT AND LOADED with flavor, this versatile dish is also good with seitan or tofu instead of tempeh, or with broccoli or asparagus in place of the green beans. Serve over hot cooked rice.

¼ cup wheat-free tamari

1 tablespoon water

1 teaspoon Asian chili paste

1 teaspoon dark sesame oil

1 teaspoon natural sugar

8 ounces tempeh, steamed (see page 6)

1 tablespoon vegetable oil or ¼ cup water

1 pound green beans, trimmed

1 small red onion, thinly sliced

3 garlic cloves, minced

1 teaspoon grated fresh ginger

½ teaspoon red pepper flakes

2 tablespoons dry sherry

Hot cooked rice, for serving

1. In a shallow bowl, combine 2 tablespoons of the tamari, the water, chili paste, sesame oil, and sugar. Mix well. Crumble or chop the tempeh and add to the bowl. Mix well, stirring to coat the tempeh. Reserve.

2. Heat the oil or water in a large skillet or wok over medium-high heat. Add the green beans, onion, and garlic, and sauté, stirring, until just tender, about 5 minutes. Add the ginger, red pepper flakes, reserved tempeh mixture, sherry, and the remaining 2 tablespoons tamari. Stir-fry until hot, 2 to 3 minutes. Serve over rice.

SERVES 4

chipotle-citrus tofu and broccoli

THE COMBINATION OF HEAT from the chipotles and citrus from the orange and lemon juices makes a flavorful sauce that packs a punch for the broccoli and tofu. This can be enjoyed alone or served over rice or quinoa; and, of course, you may substitute another vegetable for the broccoli (cauliflower or asparagus are good choices) or use seitan, tempeh, or cooked beans in place of the tofu.

3 cups small broccoli florets

1 tablespoon vegetable oil

1 pound extra-firm tofu, well drained, blotted dry, and cut into ½-inch dice

3 scallions, minced

2 garlic cloves, minced

Salt and freshly ground black pepper

⅔ cup freshly squeezed orange juice

2 chipotle chiles in adobo, pureed or finely minced

1 tablespoon tomato paste

1 tablespoon Dijon mustard

1 teaspoon natural sugar

½ cup water or vegetable broth

1 tablespoon cornstarch dissolved in 2 tablespoons water

1 tablespoon freshly squeezed lemon juice

1. Heat about an inch of water in a skillet and bring to a boil. Add the broccoli and cook until just tender. Drain and set aside in a bowl.

2. Wipe out the skillet and add the oil. Heat the skillet over medium-high heat. Add the tofu and sauté until golden brown, about 10 minutes. Add the scallions and garlic, season to taste with salt and pepper, and cook 1 minute longer, then transfer the tofu mixture to the bowl with the broccoli.

3. In the same skillet, bring the orange juice to a boil. Reduce the heat to medium, stir in the chipotle chiles, tomato paste, mustard, sugar, and water, and cook until slightly syrupy, about 5 minutes. Stir in the cornstarch mixture for about 1 minute to thicken. Add the lemon juice. Return the reserved tofu mixture and broccoli to the pan and cook until heated through and glazed with sauce, about 5 minutes. Serve hot.

SERVES 4

winter vegetable hash

Gluten-free | Soy-free

THE BEST PART OF MAKING HASH is that you never make it exactly the same way twice. Use this recipe as a guide to feature whatever vegetables or other ingredients you may have on hand. Hash is a great way to use leftover cooked potatoes or other vegetables. You can also include some chopped seitan, tempeh, tofu, or coarsely mashed beans. You can even add a little vegan cheese for some ooey-gooeyness. A drizzle of ketchup on top is classic; for something different, serve topped with a dollop of chutney or salsa.

1 tablespoon olive oil

1 large red onion, finely chopped

1 carrot or parsnip, peeled and grated

1 large Yukon gold or sweet potato, peeled and grated

½ red or green bell pepper, seeded and chopped

4 ounces cremini or shiitake mushrooms, stemmed and thinly sliced

½ teaspoon dried basil

2 tablespoons wheat-free tamari

¾ cup fresh or thawed frozen green peas

¼ cup coarsely chopped toasted walnuts

2 tablespoons minced fresh parsley

Salt and freshly ground black pepper

Heat the oil in a large skillet over medium-high heat. Add the onion, carrot, potato, and bell pepper, and sauté until softened, about 5 minutes. Add the mushrooms, basil, and tamari, and sauté for about 1 minute longer. Stir in the peas, walnuts, parsley, and salt and pepper to taste. Cook until lightly browned on the bottom, turning with a metal spatula to lightly brown on the other side. Serve hot.

SERVES 4

tempeh and cellophane noodles with lemongrass and cilantro

CELLOPHANE NOODLES ARE SO CONVENIENT to cook with because all they need is a quick soaking before adding to a recipe. If you're not a fan of tempeh, use seitan or extra-firm tofu instead.

8 ounces cellophane noodles

1 tablespoon vegetable oil

8 ounces tempeh, steamed and cut into ½-inch cubes (see page 6)

1 red bell pepper, seeded and cut into thin strips

1 medium-size zucchini, cut into matchsticks

4 scallions, minced

1 (2-inch) piece lemongrass, inner stalk only, finely chopped

3 tablespoons wheat-free tamari

1 tablespoon rice vinegar

1 teaspoon natural sugar

1 to 2 teaspoons Asian chili paste

2 tablespoons water, plus more if needed

⅓ cup chopped fresh cilantro

1. Soak the noodles in warm water until softened, about 30 minutes.

2. Heat the oil in a large skillet or wok over medium-high heat. Add the tempeh and stir-fry until browned, about 4 minutes. Add the bell pepper, zucchini, scallions, and lemongrass, and stir-fry for 1 minute. Drain the softened noodles, then add them to the skillet along with the tamari, vinegar, sugar, chili paste, and water, and stir-fry to combine and heat through. Add a little more water if the mixture seems too dry. Taste and adjust the seasonings if needed. Top with the cilantro and serve hot.

SERVES 4

couscous with edamame and chickpeas

COLORFUL AND SATISFYING, this flavorful pilaf is equally good served hot, cold, or at room temperature.

1 tablespoon olive oil or ¼ cup water

4 garlic cloves, minced

1 large carrot, peeled and shredded

6 to 8 scallions, coarsely chopped

½ teaspoon dried marjoram

¼ teaspoon red pepper flakes

1 cup fresh or frozen shelled edamame

1½ cups cooked chickpeas or 1 (15.5-ounce) can chickpeas, rinsed and drained

⅓ cup chopped reconstituted or oil-packed sun-dried tomatoes

1½ cups vegetable broth

1 cup uncooked couscous

Salt and freshly ground black pepper

½ teaspoon freshly squeezed lemon juice (optional)

¼ cup chopped fresh basil or cilantro

1. Heat the oil or water in a large saucepan over medium heat. Add the garlic, carrot, scallions, marjoram, and red pepper flakes. Sauté for 3 minutes, stirring frequently. Stir in the edamame, chickpeas, tomatoes, and ½ cup of the broth. Cook for 15 minutes.

2. Add the remaining 1 cup broth and bring to a boil. Gradually stir in the couscous, then remove from the heat and season to taste with salt and pepper. Cover and let stand for 5 minutes. Stir in the lemon juice (if using) and the basil and toss to combine. Serve hot.

SERVES 4

black beans and quinoa
with shredded vegetables

THE VEGETABLES IN THIS QUICK and colorful skillet dish can be shredded in a food processor using the shredding disk or with a box grater.

1 tablespoon olive oil or ¼ cup water

1 small red onion, shredded

1 large carrot, peeled and shredded

2 large garlic cloves, minced

2 teaspoons grated fresh ginger

1 cup uncooked quinoa, rinsed and drained

2 cups vegetable broth or water

Salt and freshly ground black pepper

1 medium-size zucchini, shredded

1 medium-size yellow squash, shredded

3 scallions, minced

1 teaspoon dried basil

1½ cups cooked black beans or 1 (15.5-ounce) can black beans, rinsed and drained

2 tablespoons minced fresh basil or Italian parsley

1. Heat the oil or water in a large skillet over medium heat. Add the onion, carrot, garlic, and ginger and sauté until the vegetables begin to soften, about 3 minutes. Add the quinoa, broth, and salt and pepper to taste, and bring to a boil. Reduce the heat to a simmer, cover, and cook for 15 minutes.

2. Stir in the zucchini, yellow squash, scallions, dried basil, and beans, and cook until the quinoa and vegetables are tender, about 10 minutes longer. Taste and adjust the seasonings if needed. Sprinkle with the fresh basil and serve hot.

SERVES 4

thai peanut bowl with tofu and asparagus

TO UNDERSCORE THE FLAVOR of the peanut sauce, sprinkle on some chopped peanuts for garnish. Thai basil adds its unique and special flavor to this dish, although you can use regular basil if Thai basil is unavailable. If asparagus is out of season, substitute green beans or broccoli (although you might want to blanch either of them first because they take longer to cook).

⅓ cup creamy peanut butter

1 tablespoon rice vinegar

3 tablespoons wheat-free tamari

1 teaspoon ketchup

½ teaspoon natural sugar

2 teaspoons Asian chili paste, or to taste

½ cup unsweetened coconut milk or almond milk

1 tablespoon vegetable oil

14 ounces extra-firm tofu, well drained, blotted dry, and cut into ½-inch dice

6 scallions, chopped

3 garlic cloves, minced

1½ teaspoons grated fresh ginger

½ cup water

1 pound asparagus, trimmed and cut into 1-inch pieces

12 cherry or grape tomatoes, halved

Cooked jasmine rice, for serving

2 tablespoons crushed unsalted roasted peanuts

2 tablespoons chopped fresh Thai basil

1. In a small bowl, whisk together the peanut butter, vinegar, 1 tablespoon of the tamari, the ketchup, sugar, and chili paste until well blended. Stir in the coconut milk, then taste and adjust the seasonings if needed. Set aside.

2. Heat the oil in a large skillet or wok over medium-high heat. Add the tofu and sauté until browned, about 7 minutes. Add the scallions, garlic, ginger, and the remaining 2 tablespoons tamari, and stir-fry for 1 minute. Remove the tofu mixture from the skillet and reserve.

3. Pour the water into the same skillet over high heat. Add the asparagus and stir-fry until just tender, about 5 minutes. Stir in the reserved tofu mixture, about half of the peanut sauce, and the cherry tomatoes, and toss gently to heat through. Serve at once over hot cooked rice. Drizzle the remaining peanut sauce over the top of each serving and sprinkle with the peanuts and basil.

SERVES 4

hoisin-glazed tofu and bok choy

Gluten-free

THREE GREAT WAYS TO MAKE this a meal: Enjoy as is; serve over cooked rice or quinoa; or roll up in a tortilla, burrito-style. Hoisin sauce, a flavorful Chinese condiment similar to barbecue sauce, adds a fragrant, spicy-sweet flavor to this dish.

¼ cup hoisin sauce

2 tablespoons wheat-free tamari

2 tablespoons water

1 tablespoon vegetable oil or ¼ cup water

2 teaspoons grated fresh ginger

3 scallions, minced

¼ teaspoon red pepper flakes

1 medium-size head bok choy, cut crosswise into thin strips

1 pound extra-firm tofu, well drained, blotted dry, and cut into ½-inch strips

2 teaspoons dark sesame oil (optional)

1. In a small bowl, whisk together the hoisin sauce, tamari, and water and set aside.

2. Heat the vegetable oil or water in a large skillet or wok over medium heat. Add the ginger, scallions, red pepper flakes, and bok choy, and stir-fry for 3 minutes. Add the tofu and the hoisin mixture and bring to a simmer, stirring gently to coat the tofu. Cook until hot, about 5 minutes. Drizzle with the sesame oil, if using. Serve hot.

SERVES 4

seitan and asparagus with orange-sesame sauce

THIS RECIPE COMBINES SEVERAL LAYERS of flavor, from sweet to hot. Be sure to taste the sauce and adjust the flavors to suit your own preference, adding more or less chili paste or red pepper flakes depending on your heat tolerance, or a little more or less agave to adjust the sweetness.

2 tablespoons tahini, peanut butter, or cashew butter

1 tablespoon agave nectar

1 tablespoon cornstarch

1 tablespoon rice vinegar

1 tablespoon wheat-free tamari

2 teaspoons dark sesame oil

2 teaspoons Asian chili paste or ½ teaspoon red pepper flakes

1 cup freshly squeezed orange juice

1 pound thin asparagus, trimmed and cut into 1-inch pieces

1 tablespoon vegetable oil

8 ounces seitan, cut into thin strips

2 garlic cloves, minced

2 to 3 scallions, minced

Hot cooked rice, for serving

1 tablespoon toasted sesame seeds or crushed unsalted roasted peanuts or cashews

1. In a small bowl, combine the tahini, agave, cornstarch, vinegar, tamari, sesame oil, chili paste, and orange juice, whisking to mix well. Set aside.

2. Pour about ½ inch of water into a large skillet or wok over high heat. Add the asparagus and cook until just tender, 3 to 4 minutes. Transfer the asparagus to a plate. Wipe out the skillet, add the vegetable oil, and heat over medium-high heat. Add the seitan and stir-fry for 2 minutes, then add the garlic and scallions and stir-fry until the seitan is browned and crispy, about 2 minutes longer.

3. Stir in the reserved sauce and cook until hot and slightly thickened, about 2 minutes. Return the asparagus to the skillet and stir gently to heat through and coat with the sauce. Serve hot over the rice, sprinkled with the toasted sesame seeds.

SERVES 4

seitan-mushroom sauté with chard and brandy sauce

BRANDY ADDS A SPECIAL FLAVOR and a touch of sophistication to this delicious sauté. It's especially good served over rice or quinoa, but you can also serve it alongside potatoes or over noodles.

1 tablespoon olive oil

8 ounces seitan, thinly sliced

1 small red onion or 2 shallots, minced

1 teaspoon tomato paste

1 cup mushroom or vegetable broth

1 tablespoon wheat-free tamari

½ teaspoon dried thyme

½ teaspoon dried basil

1 tablespoon cornstarch dissolved in 2 tablespoons water

8 ounces mushrooms (single variety or assorted), thinly sliced

⅓ cup brandy

Salt and freshly ground black pepper

6 cups stemmed chopped chard

Hot cooked rice or quinoa, for serving

1. Heat the oil in a large skillet over medium heat. Add the seitan and cook until browned on both sides, about 5 minutes. Transfer the seitan to a plate and return the skillet to the heat. Add the onion and sauté until softened, about 3 minutes. Add the tomato paste, broth, tamari, thyme, and basil, and cook, stirring frequently, for about 5 minutes.

2. Raise the heat and bring to a boil. Whisk in the cornstarch mixture, reduce the heat, add the mushrooms and brandy, and cook, stirring constantly, until the sauce has thickened and the mushrooms are tender, 2 to 3 minutes. Season to taste with salt and pepper. Add the chard, stirring to wilt. Return the seitan to the skillet and cook until heated through. Serve hot over the rice.

SERVES 4

lemony quinoa with spinach and chickpeas

Gluten-free | Soy-free

QUICK AND EASY TO MAKE yet loaded with flavor and nutrition, this tasty combo of quinoa, chickpeas, and spinach is ideal for a busy weeknight dinner.

1 tablespoon olive oil or ¼ cup water

1 small red onion, finely chopped

3 garlic cloves, minced

1 cup uncooked quinoa, rinsed and drained

1½ cups cooked chickpeas or 1 (15.5-ounce) can chickpeas, rinsed and drained

3 scallions, minced

½ teaspoon fresh or dried oregano

1¾ cups vegetable broth

Salt and freshly ground black pepper

9 ounces baby spinach, coarsely chopped

2 tablespoons freshly squeezed lemon juice

2 tablespoons minced fresh Italian parsley

1. Heat the oil or water in a large skillet or saucepan over medium heat. Add the onion and sauté for 4 minutes to soften. Stir in the garlic and sauté for 1 minute longer, then add the quinoa, chickpeas, scallions, oregano, broth, and salt and pepper to taste. Cover and cook until the quinoa is just tender, about 15 minutes.

2. Stir in the spinach to wilt, then add the lemon juice and parsley. Serve hot.

SERVES 4

pasta plus

fusilli with creamy summer vegetable sauce

PUREED FRESH VEGETABLES COMBINE to create a velvety sauce that tastes like a rich indulgence. Vary the vegetables according to your preference and their availability. If fusilli is unavailable, use your favorite pasta shape. For gluten-free, use gluten-free pasta.

1 tablespoon olive oil or ¼ cup water

1 small yellow onion, chopped

1 small red bell pepper, seeded and chopped

2 garlic cloves, chopped

1 medium-size zucchini, peeled and chopped

4 ounces white or cremini mushrooms, chopped

4 medium-size tomatoes, chopped

2 tablespoons tomato paste

1 teaspoon dried basil

½ teaspoon dried marjoram

½ teaspoon ground fennel seeds (optional)

Salt and freshly ground black pepper

1 cup cooked or canned white beans, rinsed and drained if canned

¼ to ½ cup vegetable broth or water (optional)

1 pound uncooked fusilli

2 tablespoons chopped fresh basil

1. Heat the oil or water in a saucepan over medium heat. Add the onion, bell pepper, and garlic, and cook for 5 minutes to soften. Add the zucchini, mushrooms, and tomatoes, and cook until the vegetables are soft, about 10 minutes longer. Stir in the tomato paste, basil, marjoram, fennel seeds (if using), and salt and pepper to taste. Transfer the vegetable mixture to a food processor along with the white beans, and puree until smooth. Return the mixture to the saucepan and simmer over low heat for 10 minutes to blend the flavors. Keep warm over low heat, adding a little broth or water if the sauce becomes too thick.

2. Cook the pasta in a large pot of salted boiling water, stirring occasionally, until it is al dente. Drain the pasta and return it to the pot. Add the sauce and toss to combine. Sprinkle with the basil and serve hot.

SERVES 4 TO 6

ziti with arugula-artichoke pesto

Gluten-free option | Soy-free

THE VIBRANT AND UNUSUAL PESTO made with artichoke hearts, arugula, and walnuts is tossed with white beans and cooked pasta for a satisfying one-dish meal. To make this gluten-free, use gluten-free pasta.

1 pound uncooked ridged ziti

1½ cups cannellini beans or 1 (15.5-ounce) can cannellini beans, rinsed and drained

3 garlic cloves, crushed

⅓ cup toasted walnut pieces

½ teaspoon salt

2 cups arugula

¼ teaspoon red pepper flakes

1 (6-ounce) jar marinated artichoke hearts, drained

2 tablespoons olive oil (optional)

½ cup grape tomatoes, halved lengthwise

2 tablespoons chopped fresh basil

1. Cook the ziti in a large pot of salted boiling water, stirring occasionally, until it is just tender. Drain well, reserving about ½ cup of the cooking water, and return the pasta to the pot. Add the cannellini beans and set aside, covered to keep warm.

2. While the pasta is cooking, combine the garlic, walnuts, and salt in a food processor and process until finely minced. Add the arugula, red pepper flakes, artichokes, and olive oil (if using), and process to a paste. Add a little of the reserved hot pasta water, if needed, to thin the pesto to the desired consistency.

3. Add the pesto, tomatoes, and basil to the pasta and beans and toss gently to combine. Taste and adjust the seasonings if needed. Serve hot.

SERVES 4 TO 6

penne with garlicky escarole and white beans

Gluten-free option | Soy-free

THIS FLAVORFUL DISH MADE frequent appearances on the dinner table when I was a child, where I learned early on how delicious greens could be. Another dark, leafy green such as chicory (also known as curly endive) may be substituted for the escarole. Be sure to wash the escarole extremely well before using it, as it can retain bits of grit between the leaves. To make this gluten-free, use gluten-free pasta.

2 tablespoons olive oil or ¼ cup water

5 garlic cloves, minced

1½ cups cooked cannellini beans or 1 (15.5-ounce) can cannellini beans, rinsed and drained

½ teaspoon red pepper flakes

½ teaspoon smoked paprika

½ teaspoon salt

¼ teaspoon freshly ground black pepper

½ cup vegetable broth

8 to 12 ounces uncooked penne

1 head escarole, coarsely chopped

1. Heat the oil or water in a large skillet over medium heat. Add the garlic and cook until fragrant, about 30 seconds. Add the beans, red pepper flakes, paprika, salt, and pepper. Stir in the broth and simmer for about 10 minutes to blend the flavors. Keep warm over low heat.

2. Cook the penne in a large pot of salted boiling water, stirring occasionally, until it is al dente. About 5 minutes before the pasta is done cooking, add the escarole, stirring to wilt. Drain well and return the pasta and escarole to the pot. Add the bean mixture and toss gently to combine. Taste and adjust the seasonings if needed. Serve hot.

SERVES 4

fettuccine and broccoli with almond-herb sauce

Gluten-free option | Soy-free

ALMOND BUTTER, WHITE BEANS, and fresh herbs combine to make a delectable sauce for fettuccine and broccoli. This versatile and satisfying dish can be made in one pot. Feel free to substitute another type of pasta, such as linguine or fusilli, for the fettuccine, or sub in a different vegetable, such as asparagus, for the broccoli. To make this gluten-free, use gluten-free pasta.

8 to 12 ounces uncooked fettuccine

2 to 3 cups small broccoli florets

1 tablespoon olive oil or ¼ cup water

1 small yellow onion, chopped

3 garlic cloves, chopped

1½ cups cooked cannellini beans
  or 1 (15.5-ounce) can cannellini beans,
  rinsed and drained

2 to 3 tablespoons almond butter

2 tablespoons dry white wine (optional)

½ teaspoon salt

Freshly ground black pepper

1 cup hot vegetable broth or water

¼ cup chopped fresh basil, plus whole leaves
  for garnish

1 tablespoon chopped fresh tarragon

1 tablespoon chopped fresh Italian parsley

1 tablespoon snipped fresh chives

1 teaspoon minced fresh thyme or savory

2 tablespoons sliced toasted almonds, for
  garnish

1. Cook the fettuccine in a large pot of salted boiling water, stirring occasionally, until it is tender. About 5 minutes before the pasta is done cooking, add the broccoli. Drain the cooked pasta and broccoli well and return to the pot.

2. While the pasta is cooking, heat the oil or water in a saucepan over medium heat. Add the onion and cook, stirring occasionally, until softened, about 5 minutes. Add the garlic and cook for 1 minute. Add the beans, almond butter, wine (if using), salt, and pepper to taste, and stir to blend the flavors. Transfer the mixture to a food processor or high-speed blender. Add the hot broth and half of the herbs, and puree until smooth and creamy.

3. Add the sauce to the pot with the pasta and broccoli. Add the remaining fresh herbs and toss gently to combine. Serve immediately, garnished with the almonds and whole basil leaves.

SERVES 4

one-pot cheesy mac

EVERYONE'S FAVORITE, MAC AND CHEESE, has been retooled into a one-dish meal that includes beans, nuts, and vegetables along with the creamy pasta. To make this gluten-free and soy-free, use gluten-free pasta and replace the Worcestershire sauce with coconut aminos.

8 to 12 ounces uncooked elbow macaroni or other bite-size pasta

3 cups small broccoli or cauliflower florets or chopped baby spinach or chard

½ cup raw cashews

1 cup hot vegetable broth

1 cup cooked or canned white beans, drained and rinsed if canned

⅓ cup nutritional yeast

1 ½ tablespoons freshly squeezed lemon juice

1 tablespoon Dijon mustard

1 teaspoon vegan Worcestershire sauce

1 teaspoon cornstarch

½ teaspoon onion powder

½ teaspoon garlic powder

½ teaspoon smoked paprika

½ teaspoon salt

¼ teaspoon freshly ground black pepper

½ cup cooked mashed butternut squash or canned solid-pack pumpkin

1 ¾ cups plain unsweetened almond milk

¼ cup ground toasted almonds or walnuts

2 tablespoons chopped fresh Italian parsley

1. Cook the pasta in a large pot of boiling salted water until just tender. About 5 minutes before the pasta is done cooking, add the broccoli. Drain the cooked pasta and broccoli well and return to the pot. Set aside.

2. In a food processor, combine the cashews and broth and process until smooth. Add the beans, nutritional yeast, lemon juice, mustard, vegan Worcestershire sauce, cornstarch, onion powder, garlic powder, paprika, salt, and pepper. Process until completely smooth. Add the squash and almond milk and process until smooth and creamy. Taste and adjust the seasonings if needed.

3. Pour the sauce over the pasta and broccoli in the pot and heat over low heat, stirring gently to combine and heat through, about 5 minutes. Sprinkle with the nuts and parsley and serve hot.

SERVES 4

penne and broccoli with creamy chickpea sauce

Gluten-free option | Soy-free

PUREED CHICKPEAS PROVIDE a hearty base for this easy and flavorful sauce that pairs nicely with the pasta and broccoli. Instead of broccoli, you could substitute another vegetable, such as cauliflower, asparagus, or zucchini. Use gluten-free pasta to make this gluten-free.

1 tablespoon olive oil or ¼ cup water

5 garlic cloves, chopped

8 to 12 ounces uncooked penne

3 cups small broccoli florets

1½ cups cooked chickpeas or 1 (15.5-ounce) can chickpeas, rinsed and drained

¾ cup hot vegetable broth

2 tablespoons freshly squeezed lemon juice

2 tablespoons nutritional yeast or 1 tablespoon mellow white miso paste

½ to 1 teaspoon smoked paprika

½ teaspoon dried oregano

½ teaspoon dried basil

¼ teaspoon freshly ground black pepper

Salt

1. Heat the oil or water in a small skillet over medium heat. Add the garlic and cook until softened, about 1 minute. Remove from the heat and reserve.

2. Cook the penne in a large pot of salted boiling water, stirring occasionally, until it is al dente. About 5 minutes before the pasta is done cooking, add the broccoli. Drain the cooked pasta and broccoli well and return to the pot.

3. While the pasta is cooking, combine the chickpeas and reserved garlic in a food processor. Add the broth, lemon juice, nutritional yeast, paprika, oregano, basil, pepper, and salt to taste. Process until smooth.

4. Pour the sauce over the pasta and broccoli and toss gently to combine. Serve hot.

SERVES 4

rapini and cannellini rotini

ALSO CALLED BROCCOLI RABE, rapini is an assertive green that stands up to the garlic and olives in this preparation. It is a popular vegetable throughout Italy, especially in the Puglia region. Use gluten-free pasta to make this gluten-free.

8 ounces rapini, thick stems removed

2 tablespoons olive oil

5 garlic cloves, minced

½ teaspoon red pepper flakes

½ teaspoon dried basil

Salt and freshly ground black pepper

¼ cup dry white wine or vegetable broth

1½ cups cooked cannellini beans
or 1 (15.5-ounce) can cannellini beans, rinsed and drained

⅓ cup kalamata or oil-cured black olives, pitted and halved

1 pound uncooked rotini

1. Coarsely chop the rapini. Blanch for 3 minutes in a pot of boiling salted water; remove from the pot using a skimmer or strainer, drain well, and reserve. Keep the water boiling for the pasta.

2. Heat the oil in a large skillet over medium heat. Add the garlic and cook until fragrant, about 30 seconds. Stir in the red pepper flakes, basil, and salt and pepper to taste. Add the rapini and wine and cook, stirring frequently, until the rapini is tender, about 5 minutes. Add the beans and olives and keep warm over low heat.

3. Cook the rotini in the boiling water until it is al dente. Drain the rotini and return it to the pot. Add the rapini mixture, and toss to combine. Taste and adjust the seasonings if needed. Serve hot.

SERVES 4 TO 6

spinach alfredo linguine

THIS CREAMY PASTA DISH features a rich sauce made with fresh spinach and white beans for a nutritious one-dish meal that only tastes indulgent. To make this gluten-free, use gluten-free pasta.

1 tablespoon olive oil or ¼ cup water

5 garlic cloves, chopped

9 ounces spinach, thick stems removed

1½ cups cooked white beans or 1 (15.5-ounce) can white beans, rinsed and drained

½ cup vegetable broth

Salt and freshly ground black pepper

½ cup plain unsweetened almond milk or other nondairy milk

2 tablespoons freshly squeezed lemon juice

2 tablespoons nutritional yeast or 1 tablespoon mellow white miso paste

1 teaspoon smoked paprika

1 teaspoon dried basil

1 pound uncooked linguine

1. Heat the oil or water in a small skillet over medium heat. Add the garlic and cook until softened, about 1 minute. Add the spinach and cook until wilted, 3 minutes. Stir in the beans and broth and season to taste with salt and pepper. Remove from the heat.

2. In a food processor or high-speed blender, combine the spinach mixture, almond milk, lemon juice, nutritional yeast, paprika, basil, and salt and pepper to taste. Process until smooth. Taste and adjust the seasonings if needed.

3. Cook the pasta in a large pot of salted boiling water, stirring occasionally, until it is al dente. Drain well and return to the pot. Pour the sauce over the pasta and toss gently to combine. Serve hot.

SERVES 4 TO 6

ziti with sicilian-style tomato sauce

LOOK FOR ZITI RIGATI, or ridged ziti—the chunky sauce will adhere better than it will to the smooth variety. The addition of eggplant adds hearty texture to the rich sauce and makes it distinctly Sicilian.

1 tablespoon olive oil

2 vegan sausage links, chopped (optional)

1 small yellow onion, chopped

1 small eggplant, peeled and cut into ¼-inch dice

1 small red bell pepper, seeded and cut into ¼-inch dice

5 garlic cloves, minced

3 tablespoons tomato paste

½ teaspoon dried oregano

½ teaspoon dried basil

½ teaspoon red pepper flakes

½ teaspoon natural sugar

1 (28-ounce) can diced tomatoes, undrained

1 tablespoon capers, drained

Salt and freshly ground black pepper

¼ cup chopped fresh basil or 2 teaspoons dried basil

8 to 12 ounces uncooked ridged ziti

Chopped fresh Italian parsley, for garnish (optional)

1. If using the sausage, heat the oil in a large skillet over medium heat. Add the sausage and cook until browned. Transfer the sausage to a plate and reserve.

2. Return the skillet to the stove over medium heat. Add the onion, eggplant, and bell pepper and cook, stirring occasionally, until softened, about 5 minutes. Add the garlic and a little water if needed so the vegetables do not burn. Cook for 1 minute longer, then stir in the tomato paste, oregano, ½ teaspoon dried basil, red pepper flakes, sugar, tomatoes with their juices, capers, and salt and pepper to taste, and bring just to a boil. Reduce the heat to low and simmer until the sauce has thickened and the flavors have blended, about 15 minutes.

3. Add the fresh basil and the reserved sausage, if using. Taste and adjust the seasonings if needed. Keep warm over low heat.

4. Cook the ziti in a large pot of salted boiling water, stirring occasionally, until it is al dente. Drain well and return to the pot. Add the sauce and toss gently to combine. Serve hot, garnished with parsley, if desired.

SERVES 4

fettuccine with creamy cannellini tomato sauce

GOOD-QUALITY CANNED TOMATOES are imperative to the success of this sauce—imported Italian brands tend to be the most flavorful. For a variation, skip the pureeing step and add the beans whole for more texture. To make this gluten-free, use gluten-free pasta.

1 tablespoon olive oil or ¼ cup water

1 small yellow onion, chopped

4 garlic cloves, minced

1 (14.5-ounce) can crushed tomatoes

1 (14.5-ounce) can diced tomatoes, undrained

1½ teaspoons dried basil

½ teaspoon dried marjoram

Salt and freshly ground black pepper

1½ cups cooked cannellini beans
  or 1 (15.5-ounce) can cannellini beans, rinsed and drained

8 to 12 ounces uncooked fettuccine

2 tablespoons minced fresh Italian parsley or basil

1. Heat the oil or water in a saucepan over medium heat. Add the onion and cook until softened, about 5 minutes. Add the garlic and cook for 1 minute longer, then stir in the crushed tomatoes, diced tomatoes with their juices, dried basil, marjoram, and salt and pepper to taste. Simmer the sauce for 15 minutes, stirring occasionally, to blend the flavors and reduce it slightly.

2. Puree the beans in a high-speed blender or food processor. Add the sauce and process until smooth. Return the sauce to the saucepan. Taste and adjust the seasonings if needed. Keep the sauce warm over low heat.

3. Cook the fettuccine in a large pot of salted boiling water, stirring occasionally, until it is al dente. Drain well and return to the pot. Add the sauce and toss to combine. Sprinkle with the parsley and serve hot.

SERVES 4

pasta and zucchini puttanesca

THE ADDITION OF ZUCCHINI is a departure from the traditional puttanesca sauce, but it melds well into the sauce and is a great way to enjoy more vegetables. For even more substance, you can add some sliced sautéed vegan sausage or cooked white beans to the sauce. For gluten-free, use gluten-free pasta.

1 tablespoon olive oil or ¼ cup water

5 garlic cloves, minced

2 medium-size zucchini, finely chopped

½ teaspoon red pepper flakes

2 tablespoons tomato paste

1 (14.5-ounce) can diced tomatoes, undrained

1 (14.5-ounce) can crushed tomatoes

½ cup pitted black gaeta or kalamata olives, halved

⅓ cup pitted green olives, halved or sliced

2 tablespoons capers, drained

1 teaspoon dried basil

½ teaspoon dried oregano

Salt and freshly ground black pepper

8 to 12 ounces uncooked pasta of your choice

2 tablespoons minced fresh Italian parsley

1. Heat the oil or water in a large saucepan over medium heat. Add the garlic and zucchini and cook until softened, about 3 minutes. Stir in the red pepper flakes, tomato paste, diced tomatoes with their juices, crushed tomatoes, black olives, green olives, capers, basil, and oregano. Season to taste with salt and pepper. Bring the sauce to a boil, then reduce the heat to a simmer and cook for 10 minutes, stirring occasionally.

2. While the sauce is simmering, cook the pasta in a large pot of salted boiling water, stirring occasionally, until it is al dente. Drain well and return to the pot. Add the sauce and toss gently to combine. Sprinkle with the parsley, and serve hot.

SERVES 4

rigatoni and beans with radicchio and olives

THIS SIMPLE BUT SOPHISTICATED recipe is also quite versatile. You can use sautéed seitan, tempeh, or tofu instead of the beans or substitute arugula or broccoli rabe for the radicchio. To make this gluten-free, use gluten-free pasta.

2 tablespoons olive oil or ¼ cup water or vegetable broth

1 yellow bell pepper, seeded and cut into ½-inch dice

4 garlic cloves, minced

1 small head radicchio, chopped (about 2½ cups)

⅓ cup white wine

⅓ cup vegetable broth

Salt and freshly ground black pepper

¼ cup reconstituted or oil-packed sun-dried tomatoes, cut into thin strips

1½ cups cooked black or white beans or 1 (15.5-ounce) can black or white beans, rinsed and drained

1 pound uncooked rigatoni

⅓ cup pitted kalamata olives, halved

¼ cup chopped fresh basil

1. Heat the oil or water in a large skillet over medium heat. Add the bell pepper, garlic, radicchio, wine, and broth and season to taste with salt and pepper. Cook until slightly softened, about 5 minutes. Stir in the sun-dried tomatoes and beans and keep warm over very low heat.

2. Cook the rigatoni in a large pot of salted boiling water, stirring occasionally, until it is al dente. Drain well and return to the pot. Add the radicchio mixture, the olives, and the basil, and toss to combine. Taste and adjust the seasonings, adding more salt and pepper if needed. Serve hot.

SERVES 4 TO 6

penne and chickpeas with spinach, pine nuts, and raisins

Gluten-free option | Soy-free

THE RAISINS ADD A SWEET COUNTERPOINT to the rest of the dish, especially the touch of hot red pepper. Including raisins and other sweet ingredients in savory recipes is a delicious Sicilian tradition. Adjust the amount of red pepper flakes according to your personal preference. For gluten-free, use gluten-free pasta.

8 to 12 ounces uncooked penne

2 tablespoons olive oil or ¼ cup water

5 garlic cloves, minced

9 to 12 ounces baby spinach, coarsely chopped

½ teaspoon red pepper flakes

½ cup vegetable broth

1½ cups cooked chickpeas or 1 (15.5-ounce) can chickpeas, rinsed and drained

½ cup raisins

½ teaspoon dried basil

½ teaspoon ground fennel seeds (optional)

Salt and freshly ground black pepper

¼ cup toasted pine nuts

1. Cook the penne in a large pot of salted boiling water, stirring occasionally, until it is just tender.

2. While the pasta is cooking, heat the oil or water in a large skillet over medium heat. Add the garlic, spinach, and red pepper flakes. Cook, stirring, until the spinach is wilted, about 2 minutes. Add the broth, chickpeas, raisins, basil, fennel seeds (if using), and salt and pepper to taste, and cook for 1 minute longer to blend the flavors. Keep warm over low heat.

3. Drain the cooked pasta and return it to the pot. Add the spinach mixture and the pine nuts and toss to combine. Taste and adjust the seasonings if needed. Serve hot.

SERVES 4

paglia e fieno with summer squash and lemon-basil crème

WITH PROTEIN-RICH BEANS in the luscious sauce cloaking a tasty Tuscan combo of pasta and summer squash, this is a one-dish meal that is as nutritious as it is pretty and delicious. Cut the squash into long strips using a mandoline slicer, a sharp knife, or a vegetable peeler, or use a spiralizer, if you have one. The squash strips should resemble strands of pasta. For gluten-free, use gluten-free pasta.

1½ cups cooked cannellini beans
   or 1 (15.5-ounce) can cannellini beans, rinsed and drained

½ cup vegetable broth

3 tablespoons freshly squeezed lemon juice

3 tablespoons nutritional yeast
   or 1 tablespoon mellow white miso paste

½ teaspoon garlic powder

Salt

¼ cup minced fresh basil, plus a few whole leaves for garnish

8 ounces uncooked spinach linguine

8 ounces uncooked regular linguine

1 medium-size zucchini, cut into long, thin strips

1 medium-size yellow squash, cut into long, thin strips

1. In a high-speed blender or food processor, combine the beans, broth, lemon juice, nutritional yeast, garlic powder, and salt to taste. Blend until smooth and creamy. Taste and adjust the seasonings, if needed. Stir in the minced basil and set aside.

2. Cook the linguine in a large pot of salted boiling water, stirring occasionally, until it is al dente. About 3 minutes before the pasta is done cooking, add the zucchini and yellow squash and continue to cook until the pasta and vegetables are just tender. Drain well and return to the pot. Add the sauce and toss gently to combine. Serve hot, garnished with the whole basil leaves.

SERVES 4 TO 6

fusilli with green beans and tomatoes

THE COMBINATION OF GREEN BEANS, tomatoes, and olives is typically Provençal, although the addition of pasta makes this dish decidedly Italian. It's full of flavor and deliciously satisfying as is, but feel free to add cooked white beans or sautéed slices of vegan sausage for a heartier meal. To make this gluten-free, use gluten-free pasta.

1 tablespoon olive oil or ¼ cup water

5 garlic cloves, minced

4 plum tomatoes, diced, or 1 (14.5-ounce) can diced tomatoes, undrained

⅓ cup reconstituted or oil-packed sun-dried tomatoes, cut into thin strips

Salt and freshly ground black pepper

8 to 12 ounces uncooked fusilli

8 ounces green beans, trimmed and cut into 1-inch pieces

¼ cup pitted kalamata olives, halved

3 tablespoons minced fresh Italian parsley or basil

1. Heat the oil or water in a large skillet over medium heat. Add the garlic and cook until softened, about 1 minute. Stir in both kinds of tomatoes (with the juices, if using canned) and season to taste with salt and pepper. Cook for 5 minutes to allow the tomatoes to break down a bit. Keep warm over low heat.

2. Cook the pasta in a large pot of salted boiling water, stirring occasionally, until it is al dente. About 5 minutes before the pasta is done cooking, add the green beans to the pot and continue to cook until the pasta and beans are just tender. Drain well and return to the pot. Add the reserved tomato mixture to the pasta and beans along with the olives and parsley, and toss gently to combine. Taste and adjust the seasonings if needed. Serve hot.

SERVES 4

linguine with red lentil sauce

Gluten-free option | Soy-free

ALTHOUGH LENTILS ARE MORE prominent in Indian and Middle Eastern cooking, they are also used in Italian cuisine. This thin lens-shaped legume is rich in protein, calcium, iron, and B-complex vitamins. Since lentils do not require soaking and cook up quickly, this recipe doesn't require a lot of advance planning to get dinner on the table. If you like, cook the lentils in vegetable broth instead of water. For gluten-free, use gluten-free pasta.

¾ cup dried red lentils, rinsed and picked over

2 carrots, peeled and minced

1 celery rib, minced

3 cups water

Salt

1 tablespoon olive oil or ¼ cup water

3 garlic cloves, minced

1 (6-ounce) can tomato paste

1 teaspoon dried basil

½ teaspoon dried marjoram

Freshly ground black pepper

1 pound uncooked linguine

2 tablespoons chopped fresh Italian parsley

1. Combine the lentils, carrots, and celery in a saucepan with the water and a pinch of salt and bring to a boil. Reduce the heat to a simmer and cook until tender, about 30 minutes. Drain the lentils and vegetables, reserving the cooking liquid.

2. Heat the oil or water in a large skillet over medium heat. Add the garlic and cook until fragrant, about 30 seconds. Stir in the tomato paste and cook for 2 minutes to mellow the flavor of the paste. Stir in the basil, marjoram, and reserved lentil cooking liquid, blending until smooth. Add the reserved lentil mixture and season to taste with salt and pepper. Simmer over low heat for about 5 minutes to blend the flavors. If the liquid evaporates, add a bit more water.

3. Cook the linguine in a large pot of salted boiling water, stirring occasionally, until it is al dente. Drain well and return to the pot. Add the lentil sauce and toss to combine. Sprinkle with the parsley, and serve hot.

SERVES 4 TO 6

creamy noodle curry

PASTA SEEMS TO BE COMING in all different amounts these days—I've seen packages ranging from 8 to 18 ounces! When I call for a certain amount of pasta to be used in a recipe that is less than a full package, you can either cook only the amount needed or do what I do—cook the whole amount and then use the leftover pasta another day in a different recipe. Use your choice of mild or hot curry paste or powder for this dish. Serve with a choice of condiments including chutney, chopped unsalted roasted peanuts or cashews, minced scallions, and raisins. For gluten-free, use gluten-free pasta.

1 tablespoon vegetable oil or ¼ cup water

1 medium-size onion, chopped

2 garlic cloves, minced

2 tablespoons curry paste or powder, or to taste

1 (14.5-ounce) can diced tomatoes, undrained

1½ cups cooked chickpeas or 1 (15.5-ounce) can chickpeas, rinsed and drained

4 ounces soft or silken tofu, well drained and blotted dry

1 cup low-fat unsweetened coconut milk

Salt and freshly ground black pepper

8 to 12 ounces uncooked linguine

8 ounces green beans, trimmed and cut into 1-inch pieces (about 2 cups)

1. Heat the oil or water in a large skillet over medium heat. Add the onion and cook for 5 minutes to soften. Stir in the garlic and curry paste and cook for 1 to 2 minutes, stirring to blend. Stir in the tomatoes with their juices, and simmer for 5 minutes to blend the flavors. Add the chickpeas and keep warm over low heat.

2. In a food processor or high-speed blender, combine the tofu with the coconut milk, and season to taste with salt and pepper. Blend until smooth. Stir the tofu mixture into the chickpea and tomato mixture and keep warm over low heat.

3. Cook the linguine in a large pot of salted boiling water, stirring occasionally. About 5 minutes before the pasta is done cooking, add the green beans. When the pasta and green beans are just tender, drain them well and return to the pot. Add the curried chickpea mixture and toss to combine. Serve hot.

SERVES 4

vegetable lo mein

LINGUINE STANDS IN FOR Chinese lo mein noodles in this popular noodle stir-fry. Vary the vegetables according to personal preference, substituting bok choy for the broccoli or shiitakes for the white mushrooms, if you like. For gluten-free, use gluten-free pasta.

⅓ cup hoisin sauce

¼ cup wheat-free tamari, plus more if needed

⅓ cup water or vegetable broth

1½ teaspoons Asian chili sauce

8 to 12 ounces uncooked linguine

2 cups small broccoli florets

1 carrot, peeled and thinly sliced on the diagonal

2 teaspoons dark sesame oil

1 tablespoon vegetable oil

5 scallions, minced

2 garlic cloves, minced

2 teaspoons minced fresh ginger

8 ounces extra-firm tofu, well drained, blotted dry, and cut into ½-inch dice

6 ounces white mushrooms, sliced

1. In a small bowl, combine the hoisin, tamari, water, and chili sauce. Set aside.

2. Cook the linguine in a large pot of salted boiling water until it is al dente. About 4 minutes before the pasta is done cooking, add the broccoli and carrot. Drain the pasta and vegetables and return to the pot. Add the sesame oil and toss to coat.

3. Heat the vegetable oil in a large skillet or wok over medium-high heat. Add the scallions, garlic, and ginger and stir-fry until fragrant, about 30 seconds. Add the tofu and mushrooms and stir-fry for 3 minutes. Add half of the reserved hoisin mixture and stir-fry to coat. Add the linguine and vegetables to the skillet, along with the remaining hoisin mixture. Toss gently to combine and heat through. Taste and adjust the seasonings, adding additional tamari if needed. Serve hot.

SERVES 4

pad thai tofu

THERE'S REALLY NO SUBSTITUTE for sweet-tangy tamarind paste, but if you can't obtain it, you can instead add a tablespoon or so of lime juice to the sauce and the dish will still turn out nicely. Instead of rice noodles, this dish can be made successfully using cooked fettuccine or linguine.

8 ounces rice noodles

3 tablespoons wheat-free tamari

1½ tablespoons natural sugar

2 tablespoons tamarind paste

1 tablespoon rice wine vinegar

2 tablespoons water

2 tablespoons vegetable oil

12 to 14 ounces extra-firm tofu, well drained, blotted dry, and cut into ½-inch dice

1 red onion, thinly sliced

1 carrot, peeled and cut into thin matchsticks

1 small red bell pepper, seeded and cut into thin strips

4 scallions, thinly sliced on the diagonal

4 garlic cloves, minced

1 large tomato, cut into eight wedges

½ cup fresh bean sprouts

½ cup fresh cilantro or Thai basil leaves

¼ cup chopped unsalted roasted peanuts

Lime wedges, for serving

1. Soak the noodles in hot water to soften, 10 to 15 minutes. Drain and set aside.

2. In a small bowl, combine the tamari, sugar, tamarind, vinegar, and water. Stir to mix the sauce well.

3. Heat the oil in a large skillet or wok over medium-high heat. Add the tofu and stir-fry until golden brown, about 4 minutes. Transfer the tofu to a plate.

4. Add the onion, carrot, bell pepper, scallions, and garlic to the skillet and stir-fry for 1 minute to soften the vegetables, adding a tablespoon or so of water if necessary so they don't burn. Add the noodles and stir-fry for 1 minute. Add about half of the sauce and cook, tossing to coat. Return the tofu to the skillet and add the remaining sauce. Stir-fry for a minute or two, until the ingredients are hot and coated with the sauce.

5. Top each serving with the tomato wedges, sprouts, cilantro, and peanuts, and tuck lime wedges alongside. Serve hot.

SERVES 4

hoisin tempeh noodles

Gluten-free option

NOODLE STIR-FRIES ARE COMMON to virtually all Asian cuisines; there's the lo mein of China, Thailand's pad Thai, the soba noodles of Japan, and Indonesia's bami goreng, to name a few. This recipe can be made with buckwheat soba noodles, rice noodles, or even linguine or spaghetti. To make this gluten-free, use gluten-free noodles.

5 tablespoons hoisin sauce

3 tablespoons wheat-free tamari

2 tablespoons water

2 tablespoons sake, mirin, or dry white wine (or more water)

1 to 2 teaspoons spicy Asian chili sauce

8 ounces uncooked soba noodles, rice noodles, or linguine

1 teaspoon dark sesame oil

1 tablespoon vegetable oil

8 ounces tempeh, steamed and cut into ½-inch dice (see page 6)

1 carrot, peeled and finely shredded

6 scallions, chopped

2 teaspoons minced fresh ginger

½ teaspoon red pepper flakes

1 medium-size head bok choy, coarsely chopped (about 4 cups)

2 to 3 ounces snow peas, trimmed

3 tablespoons crushed unsalted roasted peanuts

3 tablespoons minced fresh cilantro

1. In a bowl, combine the hoisin, tamari, water, sake, and chili sauce and mix well.

2. Cook the noodles according to the package directions. Drain well and return to the pot. Add the sesame oil and toss to combine.

3. Heat the vegetable oil in a large skillet or wok over medium-high heat. Add the tempeh and stir-fry quickly to brown it on all sides. Add the carrot, scallions, ginger, red pepper flakes, bok choy, and snow peas, and stir-fry for 2 minutes. Stir in the hoisin mixture and stir-fry for 2 minutes longer. Add the cooked noodles and stir-fry until heated through, about 2 minutes longer. Sprinkle with the peanuts and cilantro, and serve hot.

SERVES 4

sesame soba with tofu and broccoli

THIS SATISFYING AND DELICIOUS MEAL is loaded with protein, calcium, and vitamin C. The creamy sauce, made with tahini and sriracha, makes a good dipping sauce, too (just add less water).

1 tablespoon vegetable oil

1 pound extra-firm tofu, well drained, blotted dry, and cut into ½-inch dice

2 tablespoons wheat-free tamari

Salt and freshly ground black pepper

8 ounces uncooked buckwheat soba noodles

4 cups small broccoli florets

2 teaspoons dark sesame oil

1 garlic clove, crushed

1 teaspoon grated fresh ginger

¼ cup tahini

2 tablespoons mellow white miso paste

1 tablespoon Asian chili paste or sriracha

½ cup hot vegetable broth or water

2 tablespoons toasted sesame seeds

1. Heat the vegetable oil in a skillet or wok. Add the tofu and sauté until browned, about 5 minutes. Add the tamari and salt and pepper to taste, stirring gently to coat. Keep warm.

2. Cook the soba in a pot of boiling water according to the package directions. About 5 minutes before the soba is done cooking, add the broccoli. Drain the soba and broccoli well and rinse in cold water, then drain again and return to the pot. Add the sesame oil and toss gently to combine. Set aside.

3. In a high-speed blender or food processor, combine the garlic, ginger, tahini, miso, and chili paste, and blend until smooth. Add the hot broth and process until smooth and creamy.

4. To serve, transfer the noodles and broccoli to a large serving bowl or individual bowls. Top with the tofu and then spoon the sauce on top. Sprinkle with the sesame seeds, and serve hot.

SERVES 4

oven to table

artichoke spaghetti pie

LUSCIOUS AND LOADED WITH FLAVOR, this spaghetti pie is easy to assemble and is loaded with goodies such as artichokes, kalamata olives, and sun-dried tomatoes. To make this gluten-free, use gluten-free spaghetti.

8 ounces uncooked spaghetti

1 pound firm tofu, well drained and blotted dry

¾ cup vegetable broth

2 tablespoons dry white wine

1 tablespoon freshly squeezed lemon juice

¼ cup nutritional yeast

1 tablespoon cornstarch or tapioca starch

1 teaspoon garlic powder

½ teaspoon dried basil

Salt and freshly ground black pepper

1 (8-ounce) jar marinated artichoke hearts, drained and coarsely chopped

3 scallions, minced

¼ cup pitted kalamata olives, coarsely chopped

¼ cup reconstituted or oil-packed sun-dried tomatoes, chopped

2 tablespoons chopped fresh basil or Italian parsley

1. Preheat the oven to 375°F. Lightly oil a 10-inch springform pan or deep-dish pie plate and set aside.

2. Cook the spaghetti in a pot of boiling salted water, stirring occasionally, until it is al dente. Drain and return to the pot.

3. In a high-speed blender or food processor, combine the tofu, broth, wine, lemon juice, nutritional yeast, cornstarch, garlic powder, dried basil, and salt and pepper to taste. Process until smooth and well blended. Transfer the tofu mixture to the pot containing the cooked spaghetti. Add the artichoke hearts, scallions, olives, tomatoes, and fresh basil. Mix gently to combine.

4. Spread the spaghetti and vegetable mixture evenly in the prepared pan. Bake until firm, golden brown, and slightly puffed up, about 40 minutes. Cut into wedges and serve hot.

SERVES 4

baked rotini and arugula puttanesca

THIS IS AN EASY AND CONVENIENT WAY to get a delicious dinner on the table. If you have an ovenproof Dutch oven, you can make the whole dish in that one pot: Sauté the garlic, arugula, tomato paste, and seasonings in the pot in step 2 and remove them, then add them back in step 3. To make this gluten-free, use gluten-free pasta.

1 tablespoon olive oil

6 garlic cloves, minced

6 ounces arugula, chopped

2 tablespoons tomato paste

½ teaspoon red pepper flakes

½ teaspoon dried basil

½ teaspoon dried oregano

1 (28-ounce) can crushed tomatoes

Salt and freshly ground black ground pepper

8 to 12 ounces uncooked rotini

3 cups boiling water

1 cup cooked or canned white beans, rinsed and drained if canned

¼ cup dry white wine

½ cup pitted green olives, chopped

3 tablespoons capers

½ cup pitted kalamata olives, chopped

¼ cup minced fresh basil

1. Preheat the oven to 450°F. Heat the oil in a saucepan over medium heat. Add the garlic and arugula and cook until the garlic is fragrant and the arugula is wilted, 1 to 2 minutes. Stir in the tomato paste, red pepper flakes, dried basil, oregano, tomatoes, ½ teaspoon salt, and black pepper to taste. Keep warm over low heat.

2. Combine the rotini and water in a 3-quart baking dish. Cover tightly and put in the oven for 10 minutes. Remove from the oven, stir in the tomato and arugula mixture, cover tightly, and bake for 10 minutes longer.

3. In a high-speed blender or food processor, combine the beans, wine, ¼ cup of the green olives, and 1 tablespoon of the capers. Process until smooth and creamy.

4. Remove the pasta from the oven. Stir in the bean mixture, the black olives, the remaining ¼ cup green olives and 2 tablespoons capers, and the fresh basil. Season to taste with salt and pepper. Cover and bake for 10 minutes to heat through. Serve hot.

SERVES 4 TO 6

frittata primavera

Gluten-free

THIS COLORFUL FRITTATA makes an ideal main dish for a springtime brunch. It's an especially nice choice for a Mother's Day meal.

1 pound firm tofu, well drained and blotted dry

¾ cup vegetable broth

2 tablespoons dry white wine

1 tablespoon freshly squeezed lemon juice

¼ cup nutritional yeast

1 tablespoon cornstarch or tapioca starch

1 teaspoon garlic powder

1 teaspoon dried basil or tarragon

Salt and freshly ground black pepper

1 tablespoon olive oil or 3 tablespoons water

4 ounces thin asparagus, trimmed and cut into 1-inch pieces

4 ounces small white mushrooms, thinly sliced or chopped

5 scallions, minced

½ cup fresh or thawed frozen green peas

1½ cups cherry or grape tomatoes, halved lengthwise

2 tablespoons chopped fresh basil, tarragon, or Italian parsley

1. Preheat the oven to 375°F. Lightly oil a shallow 1½-quart baking dish or gratin dish.

2. In a food processor or high-speed blender, combine the tofu, broth, wine, lemon juice, nutritional yeast, cornstarch, garlic powder, dried basil, and salt and pepper to taste. Process until smooth and well blended. Set aside.

3. Heat the oil or water in a large skillet over medium-high heat. Add the asparagus and cook for 3 minutes. Add the mushrooms, scallions, and salt and pepper to taste, and cook for 3 more minutes. Stir in the peas and cook until all of the liquid is evaporated, about 1 minute longer.

4. Spread the cooked vegetable mixture evenly in the bottom of the prepared baking dish. Add the reserved tofu mixture and tomatoes, folding gently to combine all of the ingredients, then spread the mixture evenly in the dish. Bake until firm, golden brown, and slightly puffed up, about 40 minutes. Sprinkle with the fresh basil, cut into wedges, and serve hot.

SERVES 4

frittata puttanesca

THE BOLD FLAVORS of pasta puttanesca translate beautifully into this vegan frittata. It's great for brunch or dinner, either served on its own or accompanied by toasted Italian bread and a crisp green salad.

1 pound firm tofu, well drained and blotted dry

¾ cup vegetable broth

2 tablespoons dry white wine

1 tablespoon freshly squeezed lemon juice

¼ cup nutritional yeast

1 tablespoon cornstarch or tapioca starch

1 teaspoon garlic powder

Salt and freshly ground black pepper

⅓ cup chopped reconstituted or oil-packed sun-dried tomatoes

1 tablespoon olive oil or 3 tablespoons water

5 scallions, minced

8 ounces white mushrooms, thinly sliced or chopped

½ teaspoon dried thyme

½ teaspoon dried basil

⅓ cup pitted kalamata olives, halved

⅓ cup pitted green olives, halved

1 tablespoon capers, chopped if large

½ cup shredded vegan mozzarella cheese (optional)

1 medium-size tomato, chopped

2 tablespoons chopped fresh basil or Italian parsley

1. Preheat the oven to 375°F. Lightly oil a shallow 1½-quart baking dish.

2. In a food processor or high-speed blender, combine the tofu, broth, wine, lemon juice, nutritional yeast, cornstarch, garlic powder, and salt and pepper to taste. Add 1 tablespoon of the sun-dried tomatoes and process until smooth and well blended. Set aside.

3. Heat the oil or water in a large skillet over medium-high heat. Add the scallions, mushrooms, thyme, dried basil, and salt and pepper to taste, and cook for 3 to 4 minutes. Stir in the remaining sun-dried tomatoes, both kinds of olives, and the capers.

4. Spread the cooked vegetable mixture evenly in the bottom of the prepared baking dish. Add the reserved tofu mixture, stirring to combine all of the ingredients, then spread the mixture evenly. Sprinkle on the vegan cheese (if using) and tomato. Bake until firm, golden brown, and slightly puffed up, about 40 minutes. Sprinkle with the fresh basil, cut into wedges, and serve hot.

SERVES 4

southwestern mac and queso

Gluten-free option | Soy-free

A TASTY QUESO-LIKE SAUCE made with white beans, tomatoes, and spices makes this Southwest-style macaroni and cheese a family favorite. A green salad would make a nice addition to the meal. For gluten-free, use gluten-free pasta.

8 ounces uncooked penne or elbow macaroni

2½ cups small cauliflower or broccoli florets

1½ cups cooked white beans or 1 (15.5-ounce) can white beans, rinsed and drained

1 (10-ounce) can diced tomatoes with green chiles, undrained

3 tablespoons nutritional yeast

2 teaspoons chili powder

½ teaspoon garlic powder

½ teaspoon onion powder

½ teaspoon smoked paprika

½ teaspoon dried oregano

¼ teaspoon cayenne pepper (optional)

¼ teaspoon yellow mustard

1½ tablespoons freshly squeezed lemon juice

Salt and freshly ground black pepper

½ cup finely crushed tortilla chips

½ cup shredded vegan cheddar cheese (optional)

1. Preheat the oven to 350°F. Lightly oil a 2½-quart baking dish.

2. Cook the pasta in a large pot of salted boiling water, stirring occasionally, until it is al dente. About 5 minutes before the pasta is done cooking, stir in the cauliflower. Drain and set aside.

3. In a food processor or high-speed blender, combine the beans, tomatoes with their juices, nutritional yeast, chili powder, garlic powder, onion powder, paprika, oregano, cayenne (if using), mustard, lemon juice, and salt and pepper to taste. Process until smooth and well blended.

4. Transfer the cooked pasta and cauliflower to the prepared baking dish. Add the reserved sauce and stir to combine. Top with the crushed tortilla chips and the vegan cheese, if using. Cover and bake for 30 minutes. Serve hot.

SERVES 4

lemony quinoa-stuffed zucchini

THIS RECIPE IS LIGHT, REFRESHING, and flavorful. It's also easy to make ahead and pop in the oven, and because it is made with nutritious quinoa, white beans, and lots of veggies, it's also a satisfying one-dish meal.

4 medium-size zucchini, halved lengthwise

1 tablespoon olive oil or ¼ cup water

1 small red onion, minced

1 garlic clove, minced

1 cup uncooked quinoa, rinsed and drained

2 cups vegetable broth

4 ounces white mushrooms, chopped (about 1 cup)

1 cup cooked or canned white beans, rinsed and drained if canned

2 tablespoons minced fresh basil or Italian parsley

½ teaspoon salt

¼ teaspoon freshly ground black pepper

Juice and zest of 1 lemon

3 tablespoons ground walnuts

1. Use a grapefruit spoon or other small sharp spoon to scrape out the insides from the zucchini halves, leaving about a ¼-inch shell. Chop the zucchini flesh. Lightly steam the zucchini shells for about 3 minutes on a rack set over boiling water, and set aside.

2. Preheat the oven to 350°F. Lightly oil a large baking dish that will fit the zucchini halves in a single layer.

3. Heat the oil or water in a large saucepan. Add the onion and garlic and cook until softened, about 5 minutes. Add the quinoa and broth and bring to a boil. Reduce the heat to a simmer and stir in the mushrooms, beans, zucchini flesh, basil, salt, and pepper. Cook until the quinoa is tender, 20 to 30 minutes. Stir in the lemon juice and zest and set aside to cool slightly.

4. Spoon the stuffing into the squash halves, packing the stuffing well, then arrange them in the prepared baking dish. Cover tightly and bake until the squash is tender, about 20 minutes. Uncover, sprinkle with the ground walnuts, and return to the oven for 10 minutes to lightly brown the tops. Serve hot.

SERVES 4

turkish-style stuffed eggplant with walnut sauce

THE STUFFING HERE CALLS FOR only 1 cup of cooked grain, so it's a great way to use up any leftover cooked rice, quinoa, or bulgur. To get the most juice from a fresh pomegranate, bring it to room temperature and then roll it back and forth on a flat work surface under the palm of your hand. You can also buy bottled pomegranate juice, now available in most supermarkets. This dish may be prepared ahead of time, with the final baking completed just before serving time. Note: If you have pomegranate molasses, you can use about ⅓ cup of that instead of the pomegranate juice, lemon juice, and sugar.

2 medium-size eggplants, halved lengthwise

2 tablespoons olive oil or ½ cup water

1 large yellow onion, chopped

1 cup ground walnuts

1 cup vegetable broth

½ teaspoon ground turmeric

Salt and freshly ground black pepper

2 tablespoons tomato paste

¼ cup natural sugar

¼ cup pomegranate juice

2 tablespoons freshly squeezed lemon juice

1 small green bell pepper, seeded and chopped

1 cup cooked basmati rice, quinoa, or bulgur

2 tablespoons minced fresh mint

2 tablespoons minced fresh Italian parsley

1. Preheat the oven to 400°F. Lightly oil a baking sheet and a large baking dish that will fit the eggplant halves in a single layer.

2. Place the eggplant halves, cut sides down, on the prepared baking sheet and bake until partially softened, about 15 minutes. Remove from the oven and let cool. When cool enough to handle, scoop out the inside of the eggplants, leaving ¼-inch-thick shells intact. Coarsely chop the eggplant flesh and set aside, along with the shells.

3. Heat 1 tablespoon of the oil or ¼ cup of the water in a medium-size saucepan over medium heat. Add half of the onion, cover, and cook until softened, about 5 minutes. Add ½ cup of the walnuts, the broth, turmeric, and salt and pepper to taste. Bring to a boil, then reduce the heat to a simmer and cook, stirring occasionally, until the sauce begins to thicken, about 15 minutes.

4. In a small bowl, combine the tomato paste, sugar, pomegranate juice, and lemon juice and blend well. Add to the sauce and reduce the heat to low to keep warm while you prepare the rest of the dish.

5. Heat the remaining 1 tablespoon oil or ¼ cup water in a large skillet over medium heat. Add the remaining onion and the bell pepper, cover, and cook until softened, about 5 minutes. Stir in the chopped eggplant and salt and pepper to taste. Continue cooking to blend the flavors, about 5 minutes, then transfer the eggplant mixture to a large bowl and stir in the rice, the remaining ½ cup walnuts, the mint, and the parsley. Season to taste with salt and pepper.

6. Divide the stuffing among the eggplant shells and arrange them in the prepared baking dish. Bake until the shells are tender and the filling is hot, about 20 minutes. Serve topped with the walnut sauce.

SERVES 4

bulgur-stuffed bell peppers

Soy-free

A HEARTY STUFFING MADE with bulgur, spinach, and tomatoes makes these flavorful peppers an enticing one-dish meal. These are easy to assemble ahead of time (or even the night before) so that you can just bake and serve.

1¼ cups medium-grind bulgur

1½ cups hot vegetable broth

4 to 6 large bell peppers (any color), tops cut off and seeds removed

1 tablespoon olive oil or ¼ cup water

1 small yellow onion, minced

3 garlic cloves, minced

8 ounces chopped baby spinach, chard, or kale

1 (14.5-ounce) can fire-roasted diced tomatoes, drained and finely chopped

3 tablespoons raisins

3 tablespoons minced fresh Italian parsley

1 tablespoon minced fresh basil or 1 teaspoon dried basil

¼ teaspoon red pepper flakes

½ teaspoon salt

¼ teaspoon freshly ground black pepper

¼ cup ground walnuts

1. Preheat the oven to 375°F. Lightly oil a 2-quart baking dish and add ½ inch of water to the bottom.

2. Combine the bulgur and hot broth in a saucepan or heatproof bowl. Cover and set aside.

3. Steam the bell peppers on a rack set over boiling water in a large pot for 3 to 4 minutes to soften them slightly. Remove the peppers from the steamer and set aside, cut sides down, to drain.

4. Heat the oil or water in a large skillet over medium heat. Add the onion and cook until soft, about 5 minutes. Add the garlic and cook for 1 minute longer, then stir in the spinach, tomatoes, raisins, parsley, basil, red pepper flakes, salt, and pepper. Simmer over medium heat for 10 to 15 minutes.

5. Combine the softened bulgur with the tomato mixture and mix well. Taste and adjust the seasonings if needed.

6. Stuff the peppers with the bulgur mixture, then sprinkle with the walnuts and arrange in the prepared dish. Cover and bake until the peppers are tender, 25 to 30 minutes. Uncover and bake for 5 to 10 minutes longer to brown the walnuts. Serve hot.

SERVES 4 TO 6

japanese eggplant and tofu teriyaki

YOU CAN ADD OTHER VEGETABLES to this dish, such as portobello mushrooms and zucchini, but you may need to double the teriyaki sauce so there's enough to go around. If you have a grill, this is also delicious made with grilled vegetables.

4 small Japanese eggplants, quartered lengthwise

1 large red bell pepper, seeded and quartered lengthwise

12 ounces extra-firm tofu, well drained, blotted dry, cut into ½-inch slices, and pressed

2 garlic cloves, minced

½ teaspoon grated fresh ginger

2 tablespoons rice vinegar

2 tablespoons wheat-free tamari

1 tablespoon agave nectar or natural sugar

2 tablespoons freshly squeezed orange or pineapple juice

1 teaspoon dark sesame oil

Hot cooked rice, for serving

1. Place the eggplant quarters, bell pepper quarters, and tofu slices in a large shallow baking dish and pierce the skin of the eggplant in several places with a fork. In a small bowl, whisk together the garlic, ginger, vinegar, tamari, and agave. Add the orange juice and sesame oil, whisking constantly until blended. Pour the marinade over the vegetables and tofu, turning to coat well. Marinate, turning occasionally, for at least 1 hour at room temperature or as long as overnight in the refrigerator.

2. Preheat the oven to 400°F.

3. Place the baking dish containing the eggplant, tofu, and bell peppers in the oven and bake, turning once, until softened and lightly browned, about 30 minutes. Serve over the rice.

SERVES 4

spinach- and rice-stuffed bell peppers with almond butter sauce

THE RICH FLAVOR OF THESE STUFFED PEPPERS is enhanced by the smoky sweetness of the sun-dried tomatoes and a luxurious almond butter sauce. The rice mixture can also be used to stuff zucchini or other vegetables—or enjoyed on its own.

PEPPERS:

4 large green, red, or yellow bell peppers, tops sliced off and seeds removed

1 tablespoon olive oil or ¼ cup water

3 garlic cloves, minced

8 ounces spinach, trimmed and coarsely chopped

3 cups cooked brown rice

⅓ cup reconstituted or oil-packed sun-dried tomatoes, chopped

⅓ cup fresh chopped fresh basil or Italian parsley

½ teaspoon salt

¼ teaspoon freshly ground black pepper

SAUCE:

3 scallions, coarsely chopped

1 medium-size tomato, quartered

½ cup almond butter

1 cup hot vegetable broth

1 teaspoon dried basil

¼ teaspoon cayenne pepper

Salt

1. Preheat the oven to 350°F. Lightly oil a baking dish large enough to hold the peppers snugly.

2. *For the peppers:* Steam the peppers on a rack set over boiling water in a large pot for 3 to 4 minutes to soften them slightly. Remove the peppers from the steamer and set aside, cut sides down, to drain.

3. Heat the oil or water in a large skillet over medium heat. Add the garlic and cook for 1 minute to soften. Add the spinach and cook until the spinach is wilted, 2 to 3 minutes. Remove from the heat. Stir in the rice, tomatoes, basil, salt, and pepper and mix well.

4. Fill the peppers with the rice mixture and place upright in the prepared baking dish. Add a few tablespoons of water to the baking dish, cover, and bake until the filling is hot and the peppers are tender, 30 to 40 minutes.

5. *For the sauce:* While the peppers are baking, in a food processor or high-speed blender, combine the scallions, tomato, almond butter, broth, basil, cayenne, and salt to taste. Process until smooth. Taste and adjust the seasonings if needed. To serve, spoon the sauce over the peppers. Serve hot.

SERVES 4

cauliflower comfort bake

Gluten-free | Soy-free

THIS COZY CASSEROLE, filled with a variety of wholesome vegetables and beans, is ideal for a fall or winter meal. I like to assemble it ahead of time so it's ready to bake after a long day. A delicious fragrance fills the house as it bakes.

½ cup finely ground walnuts

1 tablespoon olive oil

1 teaspoon dried thyme

9 ounces spinach or kale, thick stems removed

1 (2½-pound) butternut squash, peeled, seeded, and cut into ¼-inch slices

1 russet potato, peeled and sliced paper-thin

Salt and freshly ground black pepper

1 medium-size head cauliflower, cored and cut into ¼-inch slices

1 cup cooked or canned white beans, rinsed and drained if canned

½ cup plain unsweetened almond milk, plus more if needed

2 tablespoons freshly squeezed lemon juice

½ teaspoon garlic powder

1. Preheat the oven to 400°F. Lightly oil a 2-quart baking dish. In a small bowl, combine the walnuts, oil, and thyme.

2. Lightly steam the spinach on the stovetop over boiling water or in the microwave, then squeeze dry and coarsely chop.

3. Spread one-third of the squash slices and one-half of the potato slices in the bottom of the prepared baking dish. Top with half of the chopped spinach and sprinkle with 1 tablespoon of the walnut mixture and salt and pepper to taste. Layer with one-half of the cauliflower slices and continue layering with the remaining squash, potato, spinach, walnut mixture, and cauliflower, ending with a layer of squash. Reserve the remaining walnut mixture. Cover and bake for 30 minutes. While the vegetables are baking, make the sauce.

4. In a food processor or high-speed blender, combine the beans, almond milk, lemon juice, garlic powder, and ¼ teaspoon salt and process until very smooth. If the sauce is too thick, add a little extra almond milk. Remove the baking dish from the oven and pour the sauce over the vegetables. Sprinkle the remaining walnut mixture over the vegetables. Cover the baking dish loosely, return it to the oven, and bake until the vegetables are tender, about 30 minutes longer. Serve hot.

SERVES 4

oven-baked indian vegetables with chickpeas

ROASTING THE POTATOES, onion, and zucchini before combining them with the spices, tomatoes, and beans adds a delicious flavor dimension to the finished dish.

3 medium-size Yukon gold potatoes, peeled or scrubbed, cut into ½-inch dice

1 small red onion, chopped

2 medium-size zucchini, cut into ½-inch dice

Salt and freshly ground black pepper

1 jalapeño chile, seeded and minced

1 teaspoon grated fresh ginger

1 tablespoon ground coriander

¾ teaspoon ground cumin

½ teaspoon paprika

¼ teaspoon ground turmeric

2 tablespoons tomato paste

1 (14-ounce) can fire-roasted diced tomatoes, undrained

1½ cups cooked chickpeas or 1 (15.5-ounce) can chickpeas, rinsed and drained

3 tablespoons chopped fresh cilantro

1. Preheat the oven to 425°F. Lightly oil two large baking pans.

2. Spread the potatoes and onion evenly in one of the baking pans and the zucchini in the second pan. Spray the vegetables lightly with cooking spray and season to taste with salt and pepper. Place both baking pans in the oven and roast for 30 minutes. Remove the pan containing the zucchini from the oven and set aside. Stir the potatoes and onions and return to the oven for 10 minutes longer.

3. Meanwhile, in a small bowl, combine the jalapeño, ginger, coriander, cumin, paprika, turmeric, and ½ teaspoon salt. Stir in the tomato paste, then add the tomatoes with their juices, stirring to blend. Remove the potatoes and onions from the oven and reduce the oven temperature to 375°F.

4. Add the zucchini to the pan containing the potatoes, then add the tomato mixture and the chickpeas and stir gently to combine. Return to the oven for 15 minutes to allow the flavors to blend and heat through. Sprinkle with the cilantro, and serve hot.

SERVES 4

spinach and quinoa tart

THE CRUST IS MADE WITH QUINOA and the filling features spinach, mushrooms, and other vegetables along with creamy white beans for a flavorful and nutritious savory tart that is terrific on its own or served with a salad.

1½ cups cooked white beans or 1 (15.5-ounce) can white beans, rinsed and drained

¼ cup plain unsweetened nondairy milk

2 tablespoons nutritional yeast

1 tablespoon almond butter

1 tablespoon cornstarch

½ teaspoon smoked paprika

½ teaspoon onion powder

½ teaspoon salt

¼ teaspoon freshly ground black pepper

1¾ cups cooked quinoa

1 tablespoon olive oil, or ¼ cup vegetable broth or water

1 small red onion, minced

4 garlic cloves, minced

9 ounces baby spinach

6 ounces white or cremini mushrooms, sliced

½ red bell pepper, seeded and chopped

¼ cup minced reconstituted or oil-packed sun-dried tomatoes

½ teaspoon red pepper flakes (optional)

1. Preheat the oven to 350°F. Spray a 9-inch pie pan with nonstick cooking spray.

2. Puree the white beans and nondairy milk in a high-speed blender or food processor. Add the nutritional yeast, almond butter, cornstarch, paprika, onion powder, salt, and pepper. Process until smooth.

3. Combine the cooked quinoa with ⅓ cup of the bean mixture and mix well to combine. Press the quinoa mixture into the bottom and up the sides of the prepared pie pan. Bake for 8 minutes, then transfer to a wire rack.

4. Heat the oil or broth in a large saucepan over medium heat. Add the onion and cook for 5 minutes to soften. Add the garlic and spinach. Cook, stirring, to wilt the spinach, for about 2 minutes. Add the mushrooms, bell pepper, sun-dried tomatoes, and 1 to 2 tablespoons water (or broth) if needed to prevent the vegetables from sticking. Add the red pepper flakes, if using, and season to taste with salt and pepper. Continue to cook until the vegetables are tender and the liquid has evaporated. Combine the remaining bean mixture with the cooked vegetables and spread the mixture evenly on top of the quinoa crust. Cover loosely and bake until firm, 30 to 40 minutes. Let cool for about 10 minutes before cutting and serving.

SERVES 4

pesto lasagna

LASAGNA IS A DELICIOUS WAY to feed a crowd—and easy, too, especially when you assemble it ahead of time. Use gluten-free lasagna noodles to make this gluten-free; either way, use regular noodles rather than the no-boil kind. The softening step below is all that's needed to prep them.

12 ounces uncooked lasagna noodles

3 garlic cloves, peeled

¼ cup pine nuts, almonds, or walnuts

2 teaspoons mellow white miso paste

1½ cups packed fresh basil leaves

Salt and freshly ground black pepper

¼ cup olive oil

1 cup cooked or canned white beans, rinsed and drained if canned

1 pound firm tofu, well drained and blotted dry

3 cups marinara sauce

1 cup shredded vegan mozzarella cheese (optional)

1. Preheat the oven to 375°F. Arrange the lasagna noodles in a 9 x 13-inch baking dish. Pour enough boiling water over the noodles to cover. Set aside to soften.

2. In a food processor, combine the garlic and pine nuts in a food processor and pulse until coarsely chopped. Add the miso, basil leaves, ¼ teaspoon salt, and ¼ teaspoon black pepper and blend thoroughly to a paste, scraping down the sides of the bowl as necessary. With the machine running, slowly pour the olive oil through the feed tube and process until well blended. Add the white beans and process until smooth. Add the tofu and pulse until combined. Season to taste with salt and pepper.

3. Drain the noodles and remove them from the baking dish. Spoon a layer of marinara sauce into the bottom of the baking dish. Top with a layer of one-third of the noodles. Spread half of the tofu mixture evenly over the noodles. Repeat with another layer of noodles, marinara sauce, and the remaining tofu mixture. Finish with a final layer of noodles and a layer of sauce. Cover tightly with foil and bake for 45 minutes. If using vegan mozzarella, uncover after baking for 40 minutes, sprinkle the mozzarella on top, and bake, uncovered, for 10 minutes longer. For either version, let stand uncovered for 5 minutes before cutting and serving.

SERVES 6 TO 8

eggplant lasagna

THIS DELICIOUS LASAGNA makes great company fare. The eggplant is especially flavorful because it is roasted before assembling the lasagna. The spinach added to the flavorful tofu mixture completes the elements needed for a well-balanced one-dish dinner. Use gluten-free lasagna noodles to make this gluten-free.

9 ounces spinach, chard, or other dark greens, thick stems removed

1 large eggplant, cut into ¼-inch thick slices

Salt and freshly ground black pepper

12 ounces uncooked lasagna noodles

1 pound firm tofu, well drained and blotted dry

¼ cup nutritional yeast

1 tablespoon mellow white miso paste

1 tablespoon freshly squeezed lemon juice

¼ cup minced fresh Italian parsley

1 teaspoon dried basil

½ teaspoon garlic powder

½ teaspoon onion powder

3 cups marinara sauce

1 cup shredded vegan mozzarella cheese (optional)

1. Preheat the oven to 400°F. Lightly oil two baking sheets or spray them with nonstick cooking spray. Lightly steam the spinach on the stovetop over boiling water or in the microwave, then squeeze dry and coarsely chop. Set aside.

2. Arrange the eggplant slices in a single layer on the baking sheets. Season to taste with salt and pepper and roast until softened, about 15 minutes, turning once about halfway through.

3. While the eggplant is cooking, place the lasagna noodles in a 9 x 13-inch baking dish. Add enough boiling water to cover, and set aside to soften.

4. While the pasta is soaking, crumble the tofu into a large bowl. Add the reserved spinach, nutritional yeast, miso, lemon juice, parsley, basil, garlic powder, onion powder, 1 teaspoon salt, and ½ teaspoon black pepper. Mix well to combine thoroughly. Taste and adjust the seasonings, adding more salt and pepper if needed.

5. Remove the eggplant from the oven and reduce the oven temperature to 375°F. Drain the softened noodles from the baking dish. Spread a layer of marinara sauce in the bottom of the baking dish. Top the sauce with a layer of one-third of the noodles. Spread half of the tofu mixture evenly over the noodles, followed by a layer of half of the eggplant slices. Top with a layer of sauce, followed by another layer of noodles and the remaining tofu mixture and eggplant. Add the last layer of noodles and end with the remaining sauce. Cover and bake until hot, about 45 minutes. If using vegan mozzarella, uncover the lasagna, sprinkle the mozzarella on top, then return the lasagna to the oven for 10 minutes, uncovered, to melt the cheese. Remove from the oven and let stand for 5 minutes before cutting and serving.

SERVES 6 TO 8

mac and thai

LEFTOVER PAD THAI was the inspiration for this macaroni pie with Thai flavors. It actually tastes like pad Thai, so I almost called it Pad Thai Pie. Instead of the white beans, you may substitute 1½ cups crumbled firm tofu, if you like. Use rice noodles to make this gluten-free.

1½ cups cooked white beans or 1 (15.5-ounce) can white beans, rinsed and drained

¼ cup plain unsweetened almond milk or other nondairy milk

2 tablespoons nutritional yeast

5 scallions, minced

2 tablespoons freshly squeezed lime juice

1 teaspoon rice vinegar

1 teaspoon peanut butter

½ teaspoon garlic powder

Salt

3 cups cooked linguine or soaked rice noodles (6 to 8 ounces before cooking)

1 tablespoon vegetable oil or ¼ cup water

½ cup chopped red onion

6 ounces asparagus, trimmed and cut into 1-inch pieces

2 garlic cloves, minced

1 small carrot, peeled and shredded

½ red bell pepper, seeded and chopped

1 cup thinly sliced white mushrooms

2 tablespoons wheat-free tamari or vegan oyster sauce

1 tablespoon natural sugar

1 teaspoon Asian chili paste (optional)

2 tablespoons water

6 grape tomatoes, halved lengthwise

3 tablespoons crushed unsalted roasted peanuts

2 tablespoons chopped fresh cilantro or Thai basil

Lime wedges, for serving

1. Preheat the oven to 350°F. Lightly oil a 9- to 10-inch pie plate or quiche pan.

2. In a high-speed blender or food processor, combine the beans, almond milk, nutritional yeast, half of the scallions, the lime juice, vinegar, peanut butter, garlic powder, and ½ teaspoon salt. Puree until smooth, then transfer to a large bowl. Add the noodles and mix well to combine. Set aside.

3. Heat the oil or water in a skillet over medium heat. Add the onion and cook for 4 minutes to soften. Add the asparagus, garlic, carrot, bell pepper, mushrooms, and remaining scallions. Stir in the tamari, sugar, chili paste (if using), and water. Cover and cook for 3 minutes. Remove the lid and continue cooking until the liquid has mostly evaporated. Transfer the vegetables to the bowl with the noodle mixture and mix well to combine. Taste and adjust the seasonings if needed.

4. Spread the mixture evenly into the prepared pan. Arrange the tomato halves on top of the mixture around the outer edge of the pan in an evenly spaced circle, pressing the tomatoes lightly into the mixture. Cover loosely and bake until bubbly, about 45 minutes. Let cool for about 10 minutes before cutting. Sprinkle the top with the peanuts and cilantro. Serve with lime wedges.

SERVES 4

tempeh and eggplant moussaka

Gluten-free option

THIS TRADITIONAL GREEK CASSEROLE made with eggplant and potatoes features tempeh to add even more heartiness. Use gluten-free bread crumbs to make this gluten-free.

1 pound russet potatoes, peeled and cut into ⅛-inch slices

1 large eggplant, peeled and cut into ¼-inch slices

1 tablespoon olive oil, plus more as needed

Salt and freshly ground black pepper

8 ounces tempeh, steamed and chopped (see page 6)

1 large yellow onion, chopped

2 garlic cloves, minced

1 tablespoon minced fresh oregano or 1 teaspoon dried oregano

¼ teaspoon ground cinnamon

⅛ teaspoon ground nutmeg

1 cup marinara sauce

12 ounces soft or silken tofu, well drained and blotted dry

1 cup cooked or canned white beans, rinsed and drained if canned

1 cup plain unsweetened almond milk

2 to 3 tablespoons freshly squeezed lemon juice

½ teaspoon garlic powder

½ cup dry bread crumbs

½ teaspoon paprika

1. Preheat the oven to 425°F. Lightly oil two baking sheets and a 9 x 13-inch baking dish.

2. Arrange the potato and eggplant slices separately on the prepared baking sheets. Lightly brush or spray the tops of the vegetables with olive oil and season to taste with salt and pepper. Bake the potato and eggplant slices until softened, about 20 minutes, turning once. Set aside. Reduce the oven temperature to 375°F.

3. Heat 1 tablespoon oil in a large skillet over medium heat. Add the chopped tempeh and cook until golden brown, about 5 minutes. Remove with a slotted spoon and reserve.

4. Add the onion to the skillet and cook until softened, about 5 minutes. Add the garlic, oregano, cinnamon, and nutmeg, and stir until fragrant, about 1 minute. Add the reserved tempeh, the marinara sauce, and salt and pepper to taste. Simmer for 10 minutes to blend the flavors. Set aside.

5. In a food processor or high-speed blender, combine the tofu, white beans, almond milk, lemon juice, garlic powder, 1 teaspoon salt, and pepper to taste. Process until smooth. Taste and adjust seasonings if needed.

6. Sprinkle a small amount of the bread crumbs evenly over the bottom of the prepared baking dish. Arrange a layer of one-third of the eggplant over the crumbs, then a layer of one-third of the potatoes, followed by half of the tempeh mixture, and another sprinkling of the bread crumbs. Add another layer of eggplant and potatoes, followed by the remaining tempeh mixture and the remaining eggplant and potatoes. Pour the tofu sauce evenly over the top and sprinkle with the remaining bread crumbs and the paprika. Bake until hot, about 45 minutes. Let rest for at least 10 minutes before serving.

SERVES 6

butternut and cremini lasagna

WILD MUSHROOMS, BUTTERNUT SQUASH, chard, and pecans make this out-of-the-ordinary lasagna an extraordinary one-dish meal. Use gluten-free lasagna noodles to make this gluten-free.

12 ounces uncooked lasagna noodles

1 tablespoon olive oil or ¼ cup water or vegetable broth

1 medium-size yellow onion, minced

1 pound butternut squash, peeled, seeded, and thinly sliced

3 garlic cloves, minced

8 ounces cremini mushrooms, sliced (about 2 cups)

6 cups chopped stemmed chard, kale, or spinach

1½ teaspoons dried thyme

Salt and freshly ground black pepper

1½ cups cooked white beans or 1 (15.5-ounce) can white beans, rinsed and drained

½ cup plain unsweetened almond milk

½ cup vegetable broth

½ cup chopped toasted pecans

¼ cup minced fresh Italian parsley

1. Preheat the oven to 375°F. Arrange the lasagna noodles in a 9 x 13-inch baking dish. Pour enough boiling water over the noodles to cover. Set aside to soften.

2. Heat the oil or water in a saucepan over medium heat. Add the onion, squash, and garlic, cover, and cook until soft, about 10 minutes. Add the mushrooms, chard, 1 teaspoon of the thyme, and salt and pepper to taste. Cook until the mushrooms are softened and the chard is wilted, about 5 minutes. Set aside.

3. Drain the noodles and remove them from the baking dish. In a food processor, combine the beans, almond milk, broth, remaining ½ teaspoon thyme, ½ teaspoon salt, and ¼ teaspoon black pepper and process until well blended. Spread a thin layer of the bean sauce in the bottom of a 9 x 13-inch baking dish. Arrange half of the noodles on top of the sauce and top with half of the squash mixture. Sprinkle with half of the pecans and half of the parsley. Top with another layer of sauce, followed by the remaining noodles and squash, and end with the sauce. Sprinkle the remaining pecans and parsley over the top, cover, and bake for 45 minutes. Uncover, and let stand for 5 minutes before cutting and serving.

SERVES 6 TO 8

vegetable paella

PAELLA IS TRADITIONALLY MADE with Spanish Valencia rice, but I use Arborio rice because it's easier to find. The saffron is traditional, but turmeric may be used instead to achieve the same golden color at a fraction of the cost. This dish is both gluten-free and soy-free without the optional vegan sausage.

1 tablespoon olive oil

1 medium-size Spanish onion, chopped

1 red bell pepper, seeded and diced

1 yellow or green bell pepper, seeded and diced

5 garlic cloves, finely chopped

1 (28-ounce) can fire-roasted diced tomatoes, undrained

3 cups vegetable broth or water

1½ cups uncooked Arborio rice

½ teaspoon ground fennel

½ teaspoon dried oregano

½ teaspoon smoked paprika

Pinch of saffron threads or ¼ teaspoon ground turmeric

½ teaspoon salt

½ teaspoon red pepper flakes

1½ cups thawed frozen or canned artichoke hearts, quartered

1½ cups cooked cannellini beans or 1 (15.5-ounce) can cannellini beans, rinsed and drained

1 cup fresh or thawed frozen peas

2 or 3 vegan sausage links, cut into ¼-inch slices (optional)

3 tablespoons chopped fresh Italian parsley

Lemon wedges, for serving

1. Preheat the oven to 375°F. Heat the oil in a large ovenproof skillet, saucepan, or paella pan over medium heat. Add the onion, bell peppers, and garlic and cook until softened, about 5 minutes. Stir in the tomatoes with their juices, broth, rice, fennel, oregano, paprika, saffron, salt, and red pepper flakes and bring to a boil. Remove from the heat, cover, and bake until the rice is tender, about 45 minutes.

2. Remove from the oven, stir in the artichokes, beans, and peas, cover, and let stand for 10 minutes before serving. If using the vegan sausages, sauté them until brown, then add to the paella. Taste and adjust the seasonings if needed. Sprinkle with the parsley and serve hot, with lemon wedges alongside.

SERVES 6

vegetable biryani

Gluten-free | Soy-free option

BIRYANI, A CLASSIC DISH of northern India, usually includes a variety of spices, vegetables, dried fruits, nuts, and basmati rice. It is traditionally baked as a layered casserole and makes a festive one-dish meal. Serve this fragrant dish with warmed naan and a spicy-sweet chutney. For soy-free, use a soy-free vegan yogurt. Note: If you don't have an ovenproof skillet, use a regular skillet on top of the stove and then transfer the biryani to a baking dish to bake.

1 tablespoon vegetable oil or ¼ cup water

1 medium-size onion, chopped

1 red or green bell pepper, seeded and diced

1 cup small cauliflower florets

1 medium-size Yukon gold potato, peeled and cut into ½-inch dice

4 ounces green beans, trimmed, cut into 1-inch pieces (about 1 cup)

2 garlic cloves, minced

1 teaspoon grated fresh ginger

1 tablespoon garam masala, or to taste

½ teaspoon ground turmeric

¾ teaspoon salt

¼ teaspoon cayenne pepper

1½ cups uncooked basmati rice

1 (14-ounce) can diced tomatoes, undrained

3 cups vegetable broth or water

1½ cups cooked dark red kidney beans or 1 (15.5-ounce) can dark red kidney beans, rinsed and drained

½ cup fresh or thawed frozen green peas

¼ cup raisins

½ cup plain vegan yogurt

Unsalted roasted cashews, for garnish

1. Preheat the oven to 375°F.

2. Heat the oil or water in a large ovenproof skillet over medium heat. Add the onion and cook until softened, 5 minutes. Add the bell pepper, cauliflower, potato, green beans, garlic, and ginger. Cook, stirring, for about 3 minutes to soften slightly. Stir in the garam masala, turmeric, salt, cayenne, and rice. Add the tomatoes with their juices and the broth and bring to a boil. Remove from the heat, and stir in the kidney beans. Cover and bake until the rice and vegetables are tender, about 45 minutes.

3. Remove from the oven, add the peas, raisins, and yogurt, and stir gently to combine. Taste and adjust the seasonings if needed. Sprinkle with the cashews and serve hot.

SERVES 4

tofu, potato, and cauliflower piccata bowl

A TRIO OF WHITE INGREDIENTS, punctuated by tomatoes and fresh herbs, combine to make a delicious meal that packs a flavor wallop thanks to the sprightly lemon sauce.

2 small Yukon gold potatoes, peeled and cut into ½-inch dice

1 head cauliflower, cored and cut into 1-inch pieces

Olive oil

Salt and freshly ground black pepper

12 ounces extra-firm tofu, well drained, blotted dry, and cut into ½-inch cubes

1 cup grape tomatoes, halved lengthwise

4 scallions, chopped

1 tablespoon capers

1½ cups cooked cannellini beans or 1 (15.5-ounce) can cannellini beans, rinsed and drained

¼ cup white wine

¼ cup hot vegetable broth

3 tablespoons freshly squeezed lemon juice

3 tablespoons nutritional yeast

½ teaspoon garlic powder

⅛ teaspoon cayenne pepper

1 tablespoon minced fresh parsley, basil, or chives

1. Preheat the oven to 425°F.

2. Arrange the potatoes and cauliflower in a single layer on two large baking sheets. Drizzle with a little olive oil or spray with nonstick cooking spray and season to taste with salt and pepper. Roast for 15 minutes, and then turn with a large metal spatula and add the tofu, tomatoes, scallions, and capers to the baking sheets. Continue roasting until the potatoes and cauliflower are tender and nicely browned, about 15 minutes longer. Season with a little more salt and pepper.

3. In a high-speed blender or food processor, combine the white beans, wine, broth, lemon juice, nutritional yeast, garlic powder, ½ teaspoon salt, and the cayenne, and blend until very smooth.

4. Divide the vegetable and tofu mixture into bowls, spoon the sauce on top, and sprinkle with the parsley. Serve hot.

SERVES 4

tetrazzini-style fettuccine

BASED ON THE GRATIN NAMED in the early twentieth century for the famous opera star Luisa Tetrazzini, this version includes the requisite sherry and almonds, while the addition of green peas provides color and makes it a satisfying one-dish meal. It's especially good accompanied by a lightly dressed green salad. To make this gluten-free, use gluten-free pasta and bread crumbs.

8 ounces uncooked fettuccine, broken into thirds

1 cup fresh or thawed frozen baby peas

1 tablespoon olive oil

3 shallots or 1 small yellow onion, minced

2 garlic cloves, minced

1 pound extra-firm tofu, well drained, blotted dry, and cut into ½-inch dice

8 ounces white mushrooms, sliced (about 2 cups)

½ cup dry sherry

Salt and freshly ground black pepper

1½ cups cooked white beans or 1 (15.5-ounce) can white beans, rinsed and drained

1 cup vegetable broth

1 cup plain unsweetened almond milk

2 tablespoons wheat-free tamari

2 tablespoons nutritional yeast

1 tablespoon freshly squeezed lemon juice

3 tablespoons chopped fresh Italian parsley

¾ cup slivered toasted almonds

½ cup vegan mozzarella cheese (optional)

¼ cup dried bread crumbs

1. Cook the fettuccine in a large pot of salted boiling water, stirring occasionally, until it is al dente. When the noodles are cooked, add the peas, then drain the pasta and peas and return to the pot. Set aside.

2. Preheat the oven to 375°F. Lightly oil a 9 x 13-inch baking dish.

3. Heat the oil in a large skillet over medium heat. Add the shallots and garlic and cook until softened, about 3 minutes. Add the tofu and mushrooms and cook until the tofu is lightly browned and the mushrooms are softened, about 5 minutes. Add the sherry, season to taste with salt and pepper, and cook, stirring, for 1 minute. Remove from the heat.

4. In a high-speed blender or food processor, combine the beans, broth, almond milk, tamari, nutritional yeast, lemon juice, and salt and pepper to taste. Process until smooth. Scoop out about 1 cup of the tofu and mushroom mixture and add it to the sauce mixture. Process until smooth. Taste and adjust the seasonings if needed.

5. Add the remaining tofu and mushroom mixture to the pot containing the pasta and peas. Add the parsley and ½ cup of the almonds, then stir in the bean-tofu sauce and mix well. Taste and adjust the seasonings if needed. Transfer the mixture to the prepared baking dish. Sprinkle the top with the vegan cheese (if using), the bread crumbs, and the remaining ¼ cup almonds. Bake, uncovered, until hot, 20 to 30 minutes.

SERVES 6

baked polenta with red beans and salsa

Gluten-free | Soy-free

THE BEAUTIFUL COLORS of bright yellow polenta, dark red beans, luscious red tomatoes, and brilliant green cilantro make this dish almost too pretty to eat. The polenta may be made a few days ahead and refrigerated until needed. To save time, you may substitute a refrigerated fresh salsa (or a bottled salsa) for the homemade version.

3½ cups water

1 teaspoon salt, plus more as needed

1 cup medium-grind yellow cornmeal

3 scallions, finely minced

2 tablespoons minced fresh cilantro

Freshly ground black pepper

1 cup Fresh Tomato Salsa (recipe follows) or other tomato salsa

1½ cups cooked dark red kidney beans or 1 (15.5-ounce) can dark red kidney beans, rinsed and drained

½ cup shredded vegan cheddar cheese (optional)

1. Bring the water to a boil in a large saucepan over high heat. Reduce the heat to medium, add the 1 teaspoon salt, and slowly whisk in the cornmeal, stirring constantly. Reduce the heat to low and continue to cook, stirring frequently, until thick, about 30 minutes. Stir in the scallions and 1 tablespoon of the cilantro, and season to taste with salt and pepper.

2. Preheat the oven to 375°F. Lightly oil a shallow 10-inch square baking dish. Spoon the polenta into the prepared baking dish and spread it evenly into the bottom. Set aside.

3. Drain any liquid from the salsa and combine half of the salsa with the beans in a bowl. Stir to combine, then spread the salsa and bean mixture over the polenta. Sprinkle with the vegan cheese, if using. Cover and bake until hot, about 20 minutes.

4. Sprinkle with the remaining salsa and remaining 1 tablespoon cilantro, and serve hot.

SERVES 4

FRESH TOMATO SALSA

Gluten-free | Soy-free

This is an easy salsa to make when ripe tomatoes are plentiful. Omit the chile if you prefer a mild salsa, or add a second one if you like it extra hot.

3 large ripe tomatoes, peeled, seeded, and chopped

1 hot red chile, seeded and minced

4 scallions, minced

1 or 2 garlic cloves, finely minced

1 tablespoon freshly squeezed lime juice

¼ cup minced fresh cilantro

Salt and freshly ground black pepper

Combine the tomatoes, chile, scallions, and garlic in a large bowl. Add the lime juice, cilantro, and salt and pepper to taste, and stir to combine. Cover and let stand at room temperature for 1 hour before serving. If not using right away, refrigerate for up to 2 days, but bring back to room temperature before serving.

MAKES ABOUT 2 ½ CUPS

polenta bake with spinach and mushrooms

THIS HEARTY AND FLAVORFUL DISH assembles easily and is ideal for preparing ahead of time and then baking when needed. If you assemble ahead and refrigerate it, either bring it to room temperature before baking or bake for a few minutes longer to be sure it is hot in the center. For an even heartier dish, add some chopped vegan sausage to the mushroom and spinach mixture (it won't be gluten-free in that case).

2 tablespoons olive oil

1 small yellow onion, finely chopped

5 large garlic cloves, minced

12 ounces cremini mushrooms, thinly sliced

½ cup dry white wine

1 tablespoon wheat-free tamari

½ teaspoon dried thyme

½ teaspoon dried basil

Salt and freshly ground black pepper

9 ounces baby spinach, coarsely chopped

6 cups vegetable broth

2 cups coarse-ground yellow polenta or cornmeal

1 cup warm marinara sauce

2 tablespoons minced fresh Italian parsley or basil

1. Preheat the oven to 375°F. Lightly oil a shallow 10-inch square baking dish.

2. Heat 1 tablespoon of the oil in a large skillet over medium heat. Add the onion and cook until softened, stirring, about 4 minutes. Add the garlic and cook, stirring, for 1 minute. Add the mushrooms and cook, stirring, until the mushrooms begin to soften, 2 to 3 minutes. Add the wine, tamari, thyme, basil, and salt and pepper to taste. Add the spinach, stirring until wilted. Cook, stirring occasionally, until the liquid is nearly evaporated, about 5 minutes. Set aside.

3. Bring the broth to a boil in a large pot over high heat. Add the polenta slowly, stirring constantly. Reduce the heat to low and stir in the remaining 1 tablespoon oil and salt to taste. Cover and cook, stirring occasionally, until thickened, about 15 minutes. Remove from the heat and let stand, covered, for 5 minutes.

4. Spoon half of the polenta into the prepared baking dish, pressing down with the back of a large spoon to form a smooth surface. Spoon the vegetable mixture on top, spreading to within a ½ inch of the edge of the polenta. Spoon the remaining polenta over the filling, spreading evenly. Smooth out the top.

5. Cover and bake for 30 minutes. Uncover and bake until the top is lightly browned, about 15 minutes longer. Remove from the oven and let rest for 10 minutes. Cut into squares and transfer to plates. Spoon warm marinara sauce over each serving and sprinkle with the parsley.

SERVES 4

white pizza with arugula pesto

EVERYONE'S FAVORITE—PIZZA—TAKES a sophisticated turn with this vegan ricotta and arugula pesto topping. The protein- and vitamin-rich beans, walnuts, and arugula make it the most fun nutritional powerhouse you'll ever eat.

DOUGH:

2 ¾ cups all-purpose flour

2 ¼ teaspoons instant yeast

1 teaspoon salt

½ teaspoon garlic powder

½ teaspoon dried oregano

½ teaspoon dried basil

1 cup lukewarm water

Olive oil

WHITE BEAN RICOTTA:

1 cup cooked or canned white beans, rinsed and drained if canned

1 garlic clove, crushed

2 tablespoons water

2 tablespoons freshly squeezed lemon juice

2 tablespoons nutritional yeast

1 teaspoon dried basil

½ teaspoon dried oregano

½ teaspoon salt

¼ teaspoon freshly ground black pepper

ARUGULA PESTO:

1 ½ cups arugula

1 cup fresh basil leaves

¼ cup fresh Italian parsley leaves

2 garlic cloves, peeled

½ cup walnut pieces, plus more for garnish (garnish optional)

2 tablespoons nutritional yeast

½ teaspoon salt

¼ teaspoon red pepper flakes

3 tablespoons olive oil

2 tablespoons freshly squeezed lemon juice

1. *For the dough:* In a large bowl, combine the flour, yeast, salt, garlic powder, oregano, and basil. Stir in the water until combined, then use your hands to knead the mixture into a soft dough.

2. Transfer the dough to a floured surface and knead until it is smooth and elastic, about 10 minutes. Shape into a smooth ball and transfer to a lightly oiled bowl. Cover with plastic wrap and let rise at room temperature until doubled in size, about 1 hour.

3. Transfer the risen dough to a floured work surface, punch it down, and gently stretch and lift to make a 12-inch round about ¼ inch thick. Transfer the dough round to a floured baking sheet or pizza stone. Use your fingertips to form a rim around the perimeter of the dough and let rise for 20 minutes.

4. Place the oven rack in the bottom position of the oven. Preheat the oven to 425°F.

5. *For the white bean ricotta:* In a food processor or high-speed blender, combine the white beans and garlic and process to a paste. Add the water, lemon juice, nutritional yeast, basil, and oregano, salt, and pepper, and blend until smooth. Transfer to a bowl and set aside.

6. *For the arugula pesto:* In the same food processor or blender (no need to wash it), combine all of the pesto ingredients and puree until smooth. The pesto should be thick.

7. *To assemble:* Bake the crust for 10 minutes, then remove from the oven. Spoon alternating dollops of the ricotta and pesto over the surface of the partially baked pizza crust, flattening each dollop with the back of a spoon—don't put too much topping in the center of the pie. Garnish the top with additional chopped walnuts, if desired. Bake until the crust is golden brown, 10 to 15 minutes longer. Serve hot.

MAKES 1 (12-INCH) PIZZA

italian deli pizza

Soy-free

HOMEMADE PIZZA IS CHEAPER than takeout and can be almost as easy when your toppings are ready-to-use Italian deli ingredients. I like to keep a stockpile of pizza dough in the freezer so that I can thaw one whenever the pizza mood strikes. No cheese is required on this flavorful pizza thanks to the protein-rich layer of flavorful chickpea spread.

DOUGH:

2¾ cups all-purpose flour

2¼ teaspoons instant yeast

1 teaspoon salt

½ teaspoon garlic powder

½ teaspoon dried oregano

½ teaspoon dried basil

1 cup lukewarm water

Olive oil

TOPPINGS:

4 ounces white mushrooms, sliced

1 (8-ounce) jar marinated artichoke hearts, well drained and quartered

½ cup pitted kalamata olives, halved

¼ cup reconstituted or oil-packed sun-dried tomatoes, chopped

1 roasted red bell pepper, chopped

½ teaspoon dried oregano

1½ cups cooked chickpeas or 1 (15.5-ounce) can chickpeas, rinsed and drained

3 tablespoons nutritional yeast

¼ teaspoon garlic powder

¼ teaspoon salt

¼ teaspoon freshly ground black pepper

3 tablespoons chopped fresh basil

3 plum tomatoes, thinly sliced

1. *For the dough:* In a large bowl, combine the flour, yeast, salt, garlic powder, oregano, and dried basil. Stir in the water until combined, then use your hands to knead the mixture into a soft dough.

2. Transfer the dough to a floured surface and knead until it is smooth and elastic, about 10 minutes. Shape into a smooth ball and transfer to a lightly oiled bowl. Cover with plastic wrap and let rise at room temperature until doubled in size, about 1 hour.

3. Transfer the risen dough to a floured work surface, punch it down, and gently stretch and lift to make a 12-inch round about ¼ inch thick. Transfer the dough round to a floured baking sheet or pizza stone. Use your fingertips to form a rim around the perimeter of the dough and let rise for 20 minutes.

4. Place the oven rack in the bottom position of the oven. Preheat the oven to 425°F.

5. *For the toppings:* Place the mushroom slices in a microwave-safe bowl. Add 1 tablespoon of water, cover, and microwave for 1 minute to soften. Drain well and transfer to a medium-size bowl. Add the artichokes, olives, sun-dried tomatoes, roasted pepper, and oregano. Stir to combine. Set aside.

6. In a food processor, combine the chickpeas, nutritional yeast, garlic powder, salt, pepper, and 1 tablespoon of the fresh basil. Process to a paste, adding up to ¼ cup water if needed to make it a spreadable consistency.

7. *To assemble:* Spread the chickpea mixture evenly on top of the pizza dough, to within ½ inch of the edge. Drain the reserved vegetable mixture of any liquid, then spoon the vegetables evenly on top of the pizza. Arrange the sliced tomatoes on top, spacing evenly. Bake until the crust is crisp and browned, 15 to 18 minutes. Sprinkle with the remaining 2 tablespoons fresh basil, and serve hot.

MAKES 1 (12-INCH) PIZZA

bahn mizza

LIKE THE BAHN MI SANDWICH that inspired it, this unusual pizza features a variety of textures, temperatures, and flavors, from the crisp hot crust and hoisin-laced tofu spread to the crunchy carrots and fresh cool cilantro. Heat-seekers may want to add extra sriracha and jalapeños.

DOUGH:

2 ¾ cups all-purpose flour

2 ¼ teaspoons instant yeast

1 teaspoon salt

1 cup lukewarm water

Olive oil

TOPPINGS:

1 large carrot, shredded

½ teaspoon natural sugar

⅛ teaspoon salt

1 tablespoon rice vinegar

2 teaspoons water

¼ cup hoisin sauce

3 tablespoons wheat-free tamari

3 teaspoons sriracha sauce, plus more if desired

1 pound extra-firm tofu, well drained, blotted dry, and cut into ¼-inch slices

3 tablespoons vegan mayonnaise

½ English cucumber, peeled and thinly sliced

2 tablespoons sliced pickled jalapeño chiles

1 cup fresh cilantro, mint, or Thai basil leaves

1. *For the dough:* In a large bowl, combine the flour, yeast, and salt. Stir in the water until combined, then use your hands to knead the mixture into a soft dough.

2. Transfer the dough to a floured surface and knead until it is smooth and elastic, about 10 minutes. Shape into a smooth ball and transfer to a lightly oiled bowl. Cover with plastic wrap and let rise at room temperature until doubled in size, about 1 hour.

3. Transfer the risen dough to a floured work surface, punch it down, and gently stretch and lift to make a 12-inch round about ¼ inch thick. Transfer the dough round to a floured baking sheet or pizza stone. Use your fingertips to form a rim around the perimeter of the dough, and let rise for 20 minutes.

4. Preheat the oven to 400°F. Lightly oil a baking sheet or line with parchment paper.

5. *For the toppings:* In a bowl, combine the carrot, sugar, salt, vinegar, and water. Cover and set aside for 30 minutes. Drain completely before using.

6. In a small bowl, combine the hoisin, tamari, and 1 teaspoon of the sriracha. Mix well. Set aside.

7. Arrange the tofu slices on the prepared baking sheet. Spread the hoisin mixture on the tofu slices and bake for 15 minutes. Remove from the oven and set aside. Increase the oven temperature to 425°F.

8. Transfer half of the tofu to a food processor or high-speed blender and process until smooth. Taste and adjust the seasonings, adding more hoisin, tamari, sriracha, or a little water, if desired.

9. Spread the pureed mixture evenly onto the pizza dough, to within ½ inch of the edge. Arrange the remaining tofu slices evenly on top of the pizza. Bake the pizza on the bottom rack of the oven until the crust is golden brown, 15 to 18 minutes.

10. While the pizza is baking, combine the mayonnaise and remaining 2 teaspoons sriracha in a small bowl, adding more sriracha if desired.

11. When the pizza is baked, cut it into 8 wedges, then drizzle with the sriracha mayo. Top with the cucumber slices, drained carrot mixture, jalapeños, and cilantro. Serve immediately.

MAKES 1 (12-INCH) PIZZA

nacho queso pizza

Soy-free

I LIKE TO USE diced tomatoes with green chiles here because they deliver a nice amount of heat. If unavailable, substitute your favorite tomato salsa (well drained) instead. Use your favorite tortilla chips as a topping for this pizza—blue corn chips look especially attractive on the pizza. If any of the queso sauce is left over, use it as a dip for chips. If you want additional heat, add some sliced pickled jalapeños along with the other toppings.

CRUST:

3 cups water

1 teaspoon salt

1 tablespoon olive oil

1 cup cornmeal

SAUCE:

1½ cups cooked white beans or 1 (15.5-ounce) can white beans, rinsed, drained, and blotted dry

1 (10-ounce) can diced tomatoes with green chiles, well drained

3 tablespoons nutritional yeast

½ teaspoon garlic powder

½ teaspoon onion powder

½ teaspoon smoked paprika

¼ teaspoon salt

¼ teaspoon yellow mustard

1 tablespoon freshly squeezed lemon juice

TOPPINGS:

¼ cup sliced pitted black olives

⅓ cup broken tortilla chips or corn chips

1 Hass avocado

¼ cup chopped fresh cilantro

1. *For the crust:* In a large saucepan, combine the water, salt, and oil, and bring to a boil. Add the cornmeal, stirring constantly with a wire whisk. Reduce the heat to medium and cook, stirring frequently, until thickened, 12 to 15 minutes.

2. Preheat the oven to 375°F. Lightly oil a round pizza pan or large baking sheet.

3. *For the sauce:* Combine the beans, tomatoes, nutritional yeast, garlic powder, onion powder, paprika, salt, mustard, and lemon juice in a high-speed blender or food processor, and process until very smooth. Taste and adjust the seasonings if needed. Set aside.

4. *To assemble:* When the polenta is cooked, spread it quickly onto the prepared pizza pan, using the oiled back of a large spoon to spread it evenly to the edge of the pan. It should be about ¼ inch thick. Bake for 12 minutes, then transfer to a wire rack.

5. Spread the sauce evenly over the crust, to within ¼ inch of the edge. Arrange the sliced olives and tortilla chips on top of the sauce. Bake until hot, about 12 minutes. When ready to serve, pit, peel, and dice the avocado. Sprinkle the pizza with the avocado and cilantro, and serve hot.

MAKES 1 (12-INCH) PIZZA

white bean cassoulet

THIS ADAPTATION OF a French country classic features white beans, an important component of the original. You may use dried beans in this recipe, if you like, but in that case it will take several hours to make, not counting the bean soaking time. By using canned beans, the cassoulet can be ready within an hour from start to finish.

2 tablespoons olive oil

1 large red onion, chopped

2 medium-size carrots, peeled and thinly sliced

2 small parsnips, peeled and chopped

3 garlic cloves, minced

2 teaspoons Dijon mustard

1 tablespoon mellow white miso paste dissolved in 2 tablespoons hot (not boiling) water

1 teaspoon dried marjoram

1 teaspoon dried thyme

1 large bay leaf

Salt and freshly ground black pepper

3 cups cooked Great Northern beans or 2 (15.5-ounce cans) Great Northern beans, rinsed and drained

1 (14.5-ounce) can diced tomatoes, undrained

1 cup vegetable broth

2 vegan sausage links, sliced and lightly browned (optional)

½ cup dry toasted bread crumbs

2 tablespoons chopped fresh Italian parsley

1. Preheat the oven to 350°F. Lightly oil a large baking dish.

2. Heat the oil in a large skillet over medium heat. Add the onion, carrots, and parsnips. Cover and cook until slightly softened, about 5 minutes. Stir in the garlic and cook until fragrant, about 30 seconds.

3. Blend the mustard into the miso mixture and stir it into the vegetables. Add the marjoram, thyme, bay leaf, and salt and pepper to taste.

4. Combine the beans and tomatoes with their juices in the prepared baking dish. Add the vegetable mixture and broth and stir to combine. Cover and bake until the vegetables are tender, about 45 minutes.

5. Uncover, remove and discard the bay leaf, and stir in the sausage, if using. Sprinkle with the bread crumbs and return to the oven to bake, uncovered, for about 10 minutes longer. Sprinkle with the parsley and serve hot.

SERVES 4

winter vegetable and pasta bake

Gluten-free option | Soy-free

WITH AN ARRAY OF COLORFUL VEGETABLES, pasta, beans, and seasonings, this comforting casserole makes an especially satisfying dinner on a cold winter evening. To make this gluten-free, use gluten-free pasta and bread crumbs.

1 medium-size red onion, chopped

1 small butternut squash (about 1½ pounds) peeled, seeded, and cut into 1-inch dice

Salt and freshly ground black pepper

9 ounces Brussels sprouts, trimmed and quartered

8 to 12 ounces uncooked penne, rotini, or other bite-size pasta

1½ cups cooked white beans or 1 (15.5-ounce) can white beans, rinsed and drained

1 (14.5-ounce) can fire-roasted diced tomatoes, undrained

1 teaspoon liquid smoke

3 tablespoons chopped fresh sage

½ teaspoon smoked paprika

½ cup vegetable broth or water

¼ cup bread crumbs or ground walnuts

1. Preheat the oven to 425°F. Lightly oil a large shallow baking pan, or spray with nonstick cooking spray, or line with parchment paper. Lightly oil a 3-quart baking dish.

2. Arrange the onion and squash in a single layer in the prepared pan. Drizzle with a little olive oil or spray with cooking spray and season to taste with salt and pepper. Roast for 15 minutes; then remove from the oven, flip the onion and squash, and add the Brussels sprouts to the baking pan. Return to the oven and continue to roast until tender, about 20 minutes longer.

3. While the vegetables are roasting, cook the pasta in a pot of boiling salted water, stirring occasionally, until it is al dente. Drain and return to the pot.

4. In a food processor, combine the beans, tomatoes with their juices, liquid smoke, half of the sage, the paprika, and salt and pepper to taste. Blend until smooth and creamy, adding as much of the broth as needed to make a pourable sauce.

5. Reduce the oven temperature to 375°F. Add the roasted vegetables to the pasta in the pot. Pour on the sauce, add the remaining sage, and mix well to combine. Taste and adjust the seasonings if needed. Transfer the mixture to the prepared baking dish and sprinkle with the bread crumbs. Bake until the top is golden, about 30 minutes. Serve hot.

SERVES 4 TO 6

chickpea pot pie

Soy-free

COMPOSED OF HEARTY CHICKPEAS and a variety of vegetables in a creamy sauce, all topped with a delicious crust, this pot pie may be the quintessential one-dish meal. If you're not a fan of chickpeas, substitute a different type of bean (cannellini is a good choice) or diced and sautéed seitan, tofu, or tempeh.

CRUST:

1⅓ cups all-purpose flour

½ teaspoon salt

½ cup vegan butter

3 tablespoons cold water

FILLING:

1 medium-size yellow onion, minced

1 large carrot, peeled and cut into ¼-inch dice

1 celery rib, minced

½ red bell pepper, seeded and chopped

3 small red potatoes, diced

6 ounces cremini mushrooms, chopped

1 tablespoon olive oil

3 cups cooked chickpeas or 2 (15.5-ounce) cans chickpeas, rinsed and drained

2 garlic cloves, chopped

2 tablespoons nutritional yeast or 1 tablespoon mellow white miso paste

½ cup vegetable broth

½ cup plain unsweetened almond milk

1 tablespoon freshly squeezed lemon juice

1 teaspoon paprika

½ teaspoon dried rosemary

½ teaspoon dried thyme

½ teaspoon dried basil

¼ teaspoon freshly ground black pepper

Salt

1 cup fresh or thawed frozen peas

1. *For the crust:* In a medium-size bowl, combine the flour and salt. Cut in the butter until crumbly. Stir in the water a little at a time, mixing to form a dough. Wrap the dough in plastic wrap and refrigerate while you make the filling.

2. Preheat the oven to 425°F. Lightly oil a 10-inch cast-iron skillet or ovenproof baking dish.

3. *For the filling:* Add the onion, carrot, celery, bell pepper, potatoes, and mushrooms to the prepared skillet; toss to combine. Drizzle with the olive oil. Roast for 20 minutes or until lightly browned, stirring once.

4. In a high-speed blender or food processor, combine 1 cup of the chickpeas with the garlic, nutritional yeast, and broth, and puree until smooth. Add the almond milk, lemon juice, paprika, rosemary, thyme, basil, pepper, and salt to taste. Blend until very smooth. Pour the sauce over the vegetables in the hot skillet. Add the remaining 2 cups chickpeas and the green peas and stir gently to combine.

5. Reduce the oven temperature to 400°F. Roll out the crust on a lightly floured surface and arrange it on top of the vegetable mixture. Bake until golden brown, 40 to 45 minutes. Let cool for 10 minutes before serving.

SERVES 4

bulgur and white bean bake with cabbage and tomatoes

THERE IS SOMETHING SO SATISFYING about the combination of bulgur, cabbage, and white beans in this stick-to-your ribs meal. If you have an ovenproof pot or Dutch oven, use it for this recipe, which makes for easier cleanup.

1 tablespoon olive oil or ¼ cup water

1 yellow onion, chopped

1 large carrot, peeled and chopped

3 garlic cloves, minced

1½ pounds savoy or napa cabbage, chopped (about 10 cups)

1¼ cups medium-grind bulgur

1½ cups vegetable broth

1½ cups cooked cannellini beans or 1 (15.5-ounce) can cannellini beans, rinsed and drained

1 (14.5-ounce) can fire-roasted diced tomatoes, undrained

1 tablespoon wheat-free tamari

1 tablespoon fresh dill or 2 teaspoons dried dill

1 teaspoon smoked paprika

Salt and freshly ground black pepper

2 tablespoons minced fresh Italian parsley

1. Preheat the oven to 350°F. Lightly oil a large (3- to 4-quart) baking dish.

2. Heat the oil or water in a large saucepan over medium heat. Add the onion and carrot and cook for 5 minutes to soften. Stir in the garlic, then add the cabbage and cook for 3 to 4 minutes longer to wilt the cabbage. Stir in the bulgur and broth and bring to a boil. Remove from the heat and transfer the mixture to the prepared baking dish. Stir in the beans, tomatoes with their juices, tamari, dill, and paprika. Season to taste with salt and pepper. Cover and bake until the liquid is absorbed and the bulgur and vegetables are tender, about 45 minutes. Sprinkle with the parsley, and serve hot.

SERVES 4

measurement equivalents

Please note that all conversions are approximate.

LIQUID CONVERSIONS		WEIGHT CONVERSIONS		OVEN TEMPERATURE CONVERSIONS		
U.S.	Metric	U.S./ U.K.	Metric	°F	Gas Mark	°C
1 tsp	5 ml	½ oz	14 g	250	½	120
1 tbs	15 ml	1 oz	28 g	275	1	140
2 tbs	30 ml	1½ oz	43 g	300	2	150
3 tbs	45 ml	2 oz	57 g	325	3	165
¼ cup	60 ml	2½ oz	71 g	350	4	180
⅓ cup	75 ml	3 oz	85 g	375	5	190
⅓ cup + 1 tbs	90 ml	3½ oz	100 g	400	6	200
⅓ cup + 2 tbs	100 ml	4 oz	113 g	425	7	220
½ cup	120 ml	5 oz	142 g	450	8	230
⅔ cup	150 ml	6 oz	170 g	475	9	240
¾ cup	180 ml	7 oz	200 g	500	10	260
¾ cup + 2 tbs	200 ml	8 oz	227 g	550	Broil	290
1 cup	240 ml	9 oz	255 g			
1 cup + 2 tbs	275 ml	10 oz	284 g			
1¼ cups	300 ml	11 oz	312 g			
1⅓ cups	325 ml	12 oz	340 g			
1½ cups	350 ml	13 oz	368 g			
1⅔ cups	375 ml	14 oz	400 g			
1¾ cups	400 ml	15 oz	425 g			
1¾ cups + 2 tbs	450 ml	1 lb	454 g			
2 cups (1 pint)	475 ml					
2½ cups	600 ml					
3 cups	720 ml					
4 cups (1 quart)	945 ml (1,000 ml is 1 liter)					

index